CRYPTO CURRENCY

BITCOIN, ETHEREUM 2.0 ALTCOINS & NFT

THE GOLDEN TICKET TO FINANCIAL LIBERATION TODAY

KAMAKIUGA

BY AUTHOR: JOHN ALO JR. / KAMAKIUGA

Table of Contents

CHAPTER 1: What is Cryptocurrency? 17

CHAPTER 2: Trading and Investing in Cryptocurrency 26

..40

CHAPTER 3: 40

Top Cryptocurrencies and Altcoins........................40

...............60

CHAPTER 4; Bitcoin as the No.1 coin 60

...............72

CHAPTER 5; Ethereum as No.2 coin 72

CHAPTPER 6; ALT coins & their performances in the crypto market 84

............107

CHAPTER 7: Decentraland (Mana) a promising ALT coin - How ATARI games are being built on this platform............107

............114

CHAPTER 8: Miners & their effects on prices and coins. 114

CHAPTER 9: Decentralized system VS Centralized system - In Contrast with FDIC traditional Banks. 125

CHAPTER 10: Regulations on Cryptocurrencies - Position of some countries on the issue {XRP to be the new Euro Digital Currency} / Blockchain concept. 130

CHAPTER 11: Concept of NFT 137

.... 149

CHAPTER 12: Wallets and External wallet devices - How to secure your Cryptocurrency from Hackers. 149

.... 152

CHAPTER 13: Coinbase/ Coinbase Pro — top Cryptocurrency brokers & How to buy, sell, convert, send and receive Crypto worldwide.......152

............162

CHAPTER 13: Own a free account today - How to Open an account with ease and get free Bitcoin for yourself and a friend. 162

DEDICATION

This book is written in Loving memory to

my Mom, 'Lita Alo'

I Love you Mom…

KAMAKIUGA / JOHN ALO JR.

Introduction

Nowadays, it seems so much like "diving" and "scattering" period for most people. Well not to worry, I am absolutely going to tell you what I meant by that trust me. But, pardon me to clarify something really fast and yet comprehensive enough to feed even the average of minds.

While growing up, I loved holding one particular thing the most. I would not just let go of it. Well, my father being a very observant person by nature, knew that part of me even before my mother could recognize it and he was always happy to give me more of it.

That particular part of me during my childhood, opened my eyes to what having more and saving more of it could do for me. I was not a genius but, I was definitely a boy of a will plus a vision and mission of liberation.

To get the truth, you have to take a risk. Not getting scared of the risk is the courage of the one seeking the truth. Do not forget that "thy shalt know the truth and the truth shall set you free".

I sought after the truth right from the stage of still being a boy. And one secret I got to know that made me continue to seek more and helping others who do not have the opportunity to seek the truth where it resides; one truth liberates one part, and brings a lift of burden, off you the seeker of truth. Meaning, you have to constantly update the truth you have known. Truth does not change by itself, time changes and once it does, truth automatically is influenced.

Truth is a secret unraveled, truth is a door that is locked, and truth is never satisfied. You have to continue looking for it. And this seeking has made many ordinary minds great. What is unknown to many, what seems impossible to many, what seems like a lie to many and what is deniable to many; has made it possible for the liberation of an ordinary mind to become a great mind. He has made the impossible possible and the lies, the truth. And, he has made a fortress just because of that.

I can imagine what is going on in your mind right now and it should most definitely be "What are you talking about? What do you want to bring out from this? Can you just get to it?

Please if I am right now, then your mind has forgotten about the two terms I used earlier "diving" and "scattering" period.

Diving literally could be in form of "descending" or undertaking enthusiastically" but, I am not about the literary meaning. Let us talk figuratively. To plunge or to go deeply into any subject, question, business, to penetrate or to explore. Without wasting your time, "scattering" is the small quantity of everything that man goes after because he sees it as a necessity. We are in this period and this period is getting really amplified due to the modern world we live in today.

Truth has led to knowledge, and knowledge, they say is power. Only few can use this power to multiply or become fruitful in and with their reasoning. Doubt has been feeding on the minds of many. Physical things can cause delusion. So, man knows that physical things attract many eyes, everything man wants to achieve are the physical things. He wants things visible to the eyes such as: standard of living, educational background, financial stability and so on.

But, if man is going to continue to think this way, there will not be any actual difference in the methods of or those things particular to how man was, is and could be in the future.

One barrier I got to know of while growing up was, I could not even spend all the money I had saved in another country apart from my country. USD was what I had and when my father took me to London, I wanted him to know how much of a man I was.

So, I took some of the money I had saved in my piggy bank along. I got to London and I wanted to buy a very appealing cupcake, I was so excited that I would use my own money to buy something for myself in London without asking my father for money. I went into the shop, and I pointed at the cupcake as I smiled from ear to ear as I stood right in front of what I was salivating for already. The baker saw the money I had in my hand and smiled as he said "this is London, pound sterling is what we spend here not dollar". I stood there so confused and asked her "where can I get the money I can spend here?"

Even as a little boy then, I knew something was still missing. Oh! God I really wished that day I could have the kind of money that had no barrier or restrictions. That same day, someone's wallet was stolen.

Anyway, my story is not to bore you but, to introduce you to what I wished for as a kid and what I always held on to as a kid. I can assure you that you are going to find this book worth your while. I have so many things to share with you. Let me say, profound or professional things to share with you.

Projections or innovations of man has been a blessing to humanity. Time flies but it leaves its prints in every passing era of man.

One of the innovations of man has triggered the pen writing on a paper. This particular innovation has caught the attention of many all over the globe and yet, many are still rejecting this innovation. The two common reasons for this are: ignorance and religious belief.

The most shocking things I have heard about this innovation is, "do not listen to them it is the devil's money and it is a sign of end time", and "it is a scam, you just wait till your money disappears all of sudden".

Truth is, I am not the kind of person that talks about religion or individual beliefs neither am I the one that runs around everywhere to shun people that bad-mouth this innovation. But I am the kind that wants to save this innovation from its killers without hurting anyone with my words or actions but, to convince people into seeing the main motive of the innovation in a very friendly manner.

My father used to say something "people are always scared of new things. But they will always find themselves craving for new things". I understood correctly what he meant even as a boy. And, I have since then taken it upon myself to look deeply into things and whatever can liberate me from being poor and still be an honest or legal source of income that I can confidently share with people. As I grew up and found what I have been looking for all these years, I decided not to stop there, I have to convince the people I can convince to see, embrace and love the new innovation.

You still do not get my drift?

To be candid, money answers to everything but, some will forever be calling out to money and money will answer them due to their ignorance or their dogmatic reasoning or way of seeing things. Oh! Please, I mean no disrespect. It is just a bitter truth that people are well aware of.

I think it is about time I revealed the name of this innovation I have been talking about and wetting the whole ground for or what do you think?

The word "Cryptocurrency" is not a new word though not all seem to be able to fathom what it means. Allow me to give an insight to its existence and originality with few words, "this is an innovation that has been around long enough for its name to ring a bell".

I want you to know that, many have written about this innovation and many will still write about it. The reason for this is, the subject is too wide and consistently becoming bigger and bigger to be neglected or overlooked.

This is a volume for you and I can promise clarity and simplicity of the subject. But the subject is just too voluminous to just be in one book.

CHAPTER 1: What is Cryptocurrency?

Now, straight to business. And, one thing I want you to know is, digitalized form of money is just the simplest meaning of what a cryptocurrency is and just as you have the paper money in your pocket or wallet at your disposal, you have your digitalized money too in your phone or any other device you want to have it on, in your digitalized wallet too. It has to be somewhere right?

A friend of mine from Kenya, staying in the States, Florida to be precise after being trained by me, he said "it is really wonderful to have lot of money and no one else can know your worth unless you show or tell them your worth yourself". You know your money is not in the bank it is in your phone or any other device mostly.

No bank charges, no SMS charges, no emails from any bank, and no bank can monitor your money not even the government. Everything is all digitalized meaning, expect swiftness in all your transaction with the aid of a working internet.

The cryptocurrency world is so fast and vast for you not to get involved in it, the more time you waste, the higher the value of the cryptocurrency will be.

A cryptocurrency is a decentralized digitalized money. In a simple sentence, there is absolutely no central computer or server.

The cryptocurrency you see, is so distributed across a network of many of computers and if you want a number, I will say thousands immediately. In the above explanation I made just now it can be easily deduced that a network without a central server is what we call a decentralized network.

One of the frequently asked questions I hear from people I have trained is, "can my money be hacked". Truth is people are scared of hackers but another truth is, your money cannot be hacked. Why?

Immediately you get yourself involved in the cryptocurrency world, you a special code is assigned to you and this special code is there for you always and acts like your personal guide preventing your information from being accessed through the internet by another user. And this is what we call cryptography.

Yeah, something is clicking already that means I am doing well. I play a lot but, we cannot all be too serious because we are talking about something serious.

Pardon me, crypto in the simplest form means hidden, and it is right there in the subject itself, "cryptocurrency". What I have been saying is, your information is well encrypted so do not be scared. You are in full control of your money. There is no involvement of a third party.

A cryptocurrency could be easily passed from a user to another user online without any interference from anyone else. Being a user means you have your account and your information has been stored successfully, that means that your physical appearance or contact is not needed to deal or before dealing with each other like banks. You deal with each other directly without needing to meet anyone. But we could make use of some trusted third parties such PayPal and the likes.

However, there are no trusted third parties in the crypto world itself. And, the essence of the trusted third parties are, being a user, you could want to use some other services that cannot or are not available in the crypto world itself as an innovation and for you to make use of these services, you have to trust a third party with your personal information.

Do not be scared, some easy to grab examples are what we do in a bank like trusting them with our money or bombarding our social media such as Facebook mostly, with our pictures and personal information.

Nonetheless, you do not have to give anyone your personal information before you can own or even use a cryptocurrency. There are no restrictions, no language barrier and there is no law against any age group and no tax is paid on its usage either.

You might have heard of the term "fiat currency" before and if not, I will explain as I have promised simplicity in this volume on the subject. Fiat currency is a term used basically by the economists and it means, any money that has an indirect market value or is given legal tender status by government fiat.

As we all know that each country has got an official currency being spent and used for all other transactions in that particular country. But, outside each of their countries, they cannot spend these different currencies. A cryptocurrency can be easily sent, received and spent all over or anywhere in the world. Remember, no restrictions whatsoever.

I told you that cryptocurrency has been around since 2009 and it was Bitcoin that was launched then. But the thing is, many do not know that has been an attempt before the successful launching of bitcoin in 2009.

Cypherpunks made an attempt to create a digital money,

Digicash and Cybercash. Those folks were smart enough to recognize that governments and corporations had much power over everyone's life. They had a very good intention, and made them attempt to use the internet to give freedom to the people of the world, allowing them to have more control moneywise and a say on their own information. As much as the vision and the mission was good, the digital money failed at the end of the nineties.

I personally think that what the Cypherpunks did was brilliant and it opened the eyes of other smart people to want to build on the idea. And when I said other smart people, I meant people like Satoshi Nakamoto. Satoshi Nakamoto created the first decentralized digital cash system after carefully studying the failure of the Cypherpunks and brought out something better from their work.

Whenever we want to talk about cryptocurrency, we have to talk about bitcoin since it became a model for every other coin were designed afterwards. To understand cryptocurrency means understanding Bitcoin.

I can say etymologically, bitcoin is gotten from "bit" and "coin". We should know that the computer language is made up of 1s and 0s, and the smaller information on a computer is referred to as "bit". What I am saying is, a bitcoin cannot exist without the computer. As it is stored in the computer.

In addition to everything we have been talking about, a decentralized cryptocurrency such as bitcoin, is now providing outlets for personal wealth for people that have gotten themselves involved in the crypto world and in such a way that this wealth is without any restriction and no one can take possession of it not even the authority.

Bitcoin is not the only cryptocurrency, there are other coins that are not bitcoin and for this they are referred to as "altcoins". "Alt" standing for the world "alternative". There are more than 5000 cryptocurrencies but Bitcoin remains the gold of all cryptocurrencies.

Bitcoin being the first peer-to-peer digital currency made the way for the altcoins. Though, many altcoins want to succeed Bitcoin by targeting the things seen as a limit on bitcoin's path for instance Bitcoin is limited to 21, so some of the altcoins have a competitive advantage against Bitcoin.

CoinMarketCap made us know that altcoins accounted for over 34% of the total cryptocurrency market as at last year February. There are a number of main altcoins and that includes the security tokens, stable coins, utility tokens and mining-based cryptocurrencies.

But I am not yet ready to go into altcoins and all right now. I have a list to follow. And, you will definitely enjoy how the whole thing is going to turn. Believing and trusting are all on hope for a better future, not relenting is the fuel to additional knowledge. You cannot stop now, neither can I stop teaching and writing on the subject.

Since we know what a cryptocurrency is now, we can go a step further to talking about how to trade or invest or both.

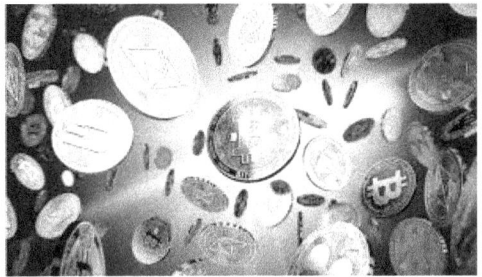

CHAPTER 2: Trading and Investing in Cryptocurrency

What is trading and what is investing?

A simple answer is, trading is buying and selling. There has to be a dealing before trading can come into the picture. Investing is when you commit your money or capital in the hope of a financial gain. We could deduce that trading is short-term as it includes serious thinking or meditating on the price movements of Cryptocurrencies. It is a higher-than-normal risk in order to obtain a higher-than-normal return kind of thing in a simple sentence. While, investing is for a long-term oriented person and it does not necessarily say that you have to be worried about taking a very high risk.

Most of the people that invest, do this to keep it like an asset that increases in price (like a fixed asset like a land) and then selling it after a long period of time such as two or three years or more based on the investor's decision. Since, it is not everyone that can wait that long, that is where "trading" comes in being the short-term one. And it is legal and there is a large number of exchanges taken place every day.

As I said earlier, the digitalized market for cryptocurrencies is decentralized, meaning that nothing in this system is issued or backed up by any authority. The system runs across a large number of computers. But there is a place for trading and investing and it is done through exchanges and then stores in digitalized wallets.

The market too is just like any other market, it is ruled by demands of people and supplies of another. Remaining free political or even economical concerns that is associated with the paper or traditional money. Uncertainties are associated with practically everything in this life including what I see as my beauty (cryptocurrency) and some of the things that can have this influencing effect on its price such as:

The supply, being the overall sum of the coins and their rates, technically, the rate of their release or getting destroyed or lost.

Just like every market you know, there will always be a capitalization of one thing or the other and in this market, I am talking about, I was referring to the value of every coin in existence or that is known at the moment and of course, how the people in the market's anticipation on any of this to be developing. The prospect is analyzed by them.

The things people say against cryptocurrency, or maybe I should just say the rumors that are defaming, people carry all around, affects the length it should go or the coverage or attention it is or had been getting.

Another one is, the occurrence bad events that could at worst cause economic setbacks or having regulatory updates. Just to mention a few.

I told you earlier that the buying and selling is done through exchanges, Coinbase one big digitalized exchange place. It is US-based exchange and it is known for its great reputation and a very sure and easy broker to use and it was established in 2012 by two partners, Brian Armstrong and Fred Ehrsam. You can easily do all your dealings without any restriction or issue with this broker/exchange. But, Coinbase is not available in some countries, making its services available to just 32 countries. And, they majorly deal in three Cryptocurrencies which are Bitcoin, Ethereum and Litecoin. Bitcoin being the one with the greatest sum of value.

Whenever you want to do any dealing through any exchange then, you have to at exchanges like Coinbase due to its reputation and exchange rate. Choosing the exchanges that require ID verification from you, whenever you are about to register there as a user, even though it is stressful I admit that too, it is the best thing trust me. Because, such exchanges, are safer, in fact, they are the safest exchanges you could deal through. They are very safe and secured than some unknown exchanges. Money is not to be wasted anyhow, before you could settle for an exchange, find out about them first. Doing your assignment on practically everything will really help you go further than the rest.

Please always choose exchanges which need some sort of ID verification from you. Even though they may take time, they are easily 100 times more safe and secure than anonymous exchanges. At the end of the day, it is your hard-earned money. You must take that extra step to keep it secured no matter what kind of risk you want to take.

Well, protecting the whole of your Cryptocurrencies, requires you having a verified digitalized wallet. This verified digitalized wallet of yours, will be the one saving all of your transactions including information such as what is called a "private key" and a "public address" making it possible for you to store, send, and even receive Cryptocurrencies from anyone you are dealing with no matter the distance or country. I know you that you might or not know what a private key and a public address are.

A private key authenticates or grants or verifies you as the one with the whole right to accessing or sending your money or both without any interference or anyone challenging you on your money.

While a public address is, the address you give out to the person or people you are dealing with and it is where everyone will be able to send you money without it getting stuck or going into any other person's address because all addresses are uniquely generated by your digitalized wallet.

Private key is yours only and it is not for you to share with anyone else. But a public address can be given to all dealers or anyone that wants to send you money without them gaining access to your money at all.

There are trading platforms and can be seen an instrument too and they are called contract for difference (CFD). Just as I said, they are essentially viewed as an instrument and are good and known as some sort of a portal for investors to go into the financial markets.

Here brokers are available and other common assets that

people involved in Forex (FX) are very familiar with. A contract for difference is said to be a type of an imitative trading that is, modelled after another thing such as gaining their own value from the onward or downward movements of the basic assets.

A trader can choose to trade contract for difference (CFD) whenever the trader wants be in a contract that involves himself or herself and the broker. Then the contract for difference (CFD) is now going to be like this in a simple sentence, the trader (the one meeting the demand of another person making the person, the seller), the broker (the platform you are using for your dealings as a trader) and the one buying (the buyer is the one requesting or demanding for what you have) all in the accord of the on examination of the prices of assets based on the market conditions.

I need you to take note of something very crucial at this point, traders can go ahead showing their enhanced reasoning or meditating skills on financial tools, there is still a difference between this type of trading and the traditional trading style.

Contract for difference (CFD), gives a room for traders to trade on the price movement of assets without the traders really owning the fundamental assets. And the thing here is, by not actually owning the fundamental assets, the contract for difference (CFD) traders can avoid some of the demerits and costs of traditional trading.

Whenever it comes to you trying to calculate what your profit or loss is, you can easily get the answer by writing out the difference between the amount at which you got in and the amount when you exited, times that by the number of contracts for difference (CFD) units. Another thing is, contract for difference (CFD) is so available across a very large number of markets.

A digitalized market for Cryptocurrencies, is where I love the most I must confess. It is an interesting place for me. And, it is the field where all great minds meet without having any physical contact with anyone of them.

The most exciting thing about it is, being a trader, you can make lot of money and then lose it all without having any physical contact with the people you are losing to at all. You can gather lot of Cryptocurrencies overnight and then lose it like a flash.

That is the reason why people take time to learn about trading and still updating the knowledge they have on Cryptocurrency trading. So many rookies in the market lose awfully and they tend to lose so much more as they fail to realize that in the market you have to learn, be patient and try the trading with what they can afford to lose.

It is a way most of us got better with time. We gained more knowledge and confidence through our individual experiences which did not come overnight either.

The best advice I can give anyone is, trading your Cryptocurrencies should not be only on the basis or with the mind of getting rich immediately.

Trading our Cryptocurrencies help the system to be busy with the meeting up of demands and supply and finally causing an increment in the price of such an asset you are trading with and the other Cryptocurrencies in the digitalized market.

Remember I told you that trading your Cryptocurrency is a case of nothing ventured, nothing wins and nothing ventured, nothing lost. Trading Cryptocurrencies, make sure that you get passive income.

I must confess, the first part of trading that you can find threatening or frightening is immediately you go into the broker/exchange you want to use, and you start seeing the graphs and lines. When I began trading as a newbie, I did not even bother reading all the graphs, instead, I went directly to buying and selling of Cryptocurrencies' aspect of the exchange. But you do not have to repeat my own mistake. There are some prominent charts you will also meet once you come into the market as a novice but, I will talk to you about some right now.

The Japanese candlestick charts being the most popular of all charts. This chart has each of its candles showing the price movement of the asset during a particular time frame.

The candles have both bodies and with their noticeable shadows. The body is concerned with showing us the difference existing between the opening price of assets and the closing price of assets.

While the obtrusive shadows show us the high or low level of our opening and our closing prices of an asset have actually gone. The chart is always colorful as it shows two colors which are green and red. whenever a green candle, the upper shadow, is showing. For instance, it is simply indicating the close price and the lower shadow of the colors green candle, indicates the open price of an asset or assets.

Whenever you need a chart that can clearly show you without any technicality, where the digitalized market turned, assisting us in identifying the distinct sequence and finally making it possible to foretell how the market will actuate.

Another one is, Relative Strength Index (RSI). This is used by traders to calculate the strength and the swiftness of any market price movement through the comparison of current price of any Cryptocurrency to its previous performance. Comparing the degree of current gains to current losses in order to know if a Cryptocurrency has been overbought or facing a condition where there have been significant trading driving prices down to lower levels, levels which seem overextended or excessive on a short-term basis, that is basically how it works.

RSI – Relative Strength Index indicate Bullish Signals

There is actually a formula for it and having a pretty look like this:

RSI = 100 - (100/(1-RS))

With the rate at which time is changing things, we really do not need to be concerned about making calculations for anything at all, because right now, the exchange you are using, will do it for you right there.

There are some popular exchanges and they are:

Coinbase is so beginner-friendly and it is the kind of exchange that it allows buying of Cryptocurrencies with USD.

Binance is another exchange offering a number greater than two hundred crypto trading pairs, making the most popular exchange in the world.

For advanced or the experienced traders that want to up their trading games, BitMEX is the exact place for you to go to trust me. It is operated by professional algo-traders, developers, and even economists, it does sound busy right?

Yeah, it a very busy exchange.

I mentioned CoinMarketCap earlier. CoinMarketCap is a site that can also be viewed as a very useful tool for all traders that are interested in having a or any caption of different Cryptocurrencies' performance. There is always a ranking of all the Cryptocurrencies by this site and on this site and it so much helps a trader in knowing the value of any Cryptocurrency. See it as a tool of indication for traders all around the world.

CHAPTER 3:

Top Cryptocurrencies and Altcoins

I have given an insight into this already so I think the best thing we can do is built on it from where we stopped.

We can easily guess number one of the top Cryptocurrencies without blinking our eyes or racking our brains at least it could be guessed to an extent.

I remember what one of my teachers used to do when I was

in my junior year, he used to say "for every new topic any good teacher wants to introduce to his or her students, a recap of everything that has been said before is highly required". I have been sticking to this advice because, I remember it always.

So, how about we have a little revision but not too much?

I told you a simple meaning of a Cryptocurrency and an altcoin. Ok let us try adding to the initial meaning. A cryptocurrency being a virtual or a digitalized money that could tokens or coins.

Probably, you have somehow seen some of the cryptocurrencies

manifesting in this real world with credit cards and you want to punch me right in the face because, you feel like I am saying nonsense.

Pardon me, I joke a lot. Let me tell you something really fast, it is true that the virtual money is finding a way to become real in the real world too but, not all can but, to be in a safer side, then I will say "not all can, yet"

We already know that the "crypto" is a very convoluted cryptography designed just for the creation and the processing of the digitalized money or currencies including the whole transactions across the decentralized system. Technically, cryptocurrencies are fully formed as codes by the teams given the responsibility to create them through the procedure called mining, and other controls they deem necessary to use.

The digital or virtual money are designed to always be with freedom as the main goal is for cryptocurrencies to be seen a code or symbol of emancipation from the manipulation and control of external bodies such as the government.

I love being simple, it gives me joy to write with simplicity and care encoded in my words. Let us talk about the altcoins too.

As I said earlier, all digitalized money that is not Bitcoin, are altcoins. They are all modelled after Bitcoin and sporadically these virtual money is referred to as "shift coins" by some people and on some sites but, I stick to calling them altcoins.

These altcoins that are being created over the years, have mostly projected themselves pretty well with some appealing characteristics that the pioneer of the crypto world does not have. They seem to look like an improved version of Bitcoin but, none of them has got a matching security level in their networks like Bitcoin's.

The cryptocurrencies we have now are more than five thousand and some have so much popularity that that others are drowned by their shadows and thereby having a very low trading volume. Some of the cryptocurrencies having so much fame today is due to big investors investing massively in them and thereby increasing their trading volume.

The coast of cryptocurrencies keeps enlarging, as more cryptocurrencies are created and you can hear that another wonderful cryptocurrency with great and attractive features has been released tomorrow just after one was released few months prior to the time the new one was released.

Despite the fact that Bitcoin is the first of its kind of the cryptocurrency world, it should not be so kind to you that analysts have come up with different methods to draw conclusions from examining tokens instead of Bitcoin. It is a thing happening frequently, for example, whenever any importance is to be given to any coin so as to rank them above one another in terms of the digitalized market cap. So, what I am saying indirectly is this, digital tokens also feature among the top cryptocurrencies' list, and some of them will or may sound pretty strange to you. The example is just not just the only known reason for tokens being of any importance. The list changes and it could still change even before dusk, fingers crossed.

Bitcoin (BTC), cannot be taken away whenever anyone wants to talk about the digital money that has the largest portion of the digitalized market for cryptocurrencies. Bitcoin has really grown in value over the years, and it is still growing in value. But other cryptocurrencies are really striving to keep themselves positioned in a very noticeable position, and they are growing really fast too in value and in popularity.

Within the space of few months, a lot of these digital

money have actually suddenly and rapidly increased in value, and quantity before they dropping swiftly again. The falling of the pioneer of the cryptocurrency world, always have an effect on the altcoins value too. And some find it a little bit or very hard leveling off.

When it comes to the cryptocurrency world, the digitalized or virtual money world or should I say sphere?

Anyhow, I will put it out in a simple way. The cryptocurrency world or realm or sphere is full of ups and downs. The cryptocurrencies are so volatile. The ups and downs of the cryptocurrencies, also lead to ups and downs of wealth of the investors of such cryptocurrencies. It is a normal happening, we all are aware that there are two times in this life, which are the good and the bad times. So, do not let that be a worry because the ups in the cryptocurrency world is way too pretty to make you feel ugly during the downs. The largest digital money will always make you feel pretty always even when it is rough. And, the utter list of the largest digital money by market cap are as follows:

The list cannot be written without the acknowledgement of the king of the cryptocurrencies, the leader and the original. The first in the space, and the portal

master. CoinMarketCap says "There are about 17.1 million Bitcoin (BTC) flowing through the network"

The one with the fingers crossed on the market capitalization on every digital market caption. With a known price per coin of over $55 thousand. The cryptocurrency I am talking about is none other than Bitcoin (BTC). And, it is not just the trending cryptocurrency, it is not just a cryptocurrency that other cryptocurrencies are modelled after or formed on a decentralized peer-to-peer network, it has set a standard for all altcoins and it has lot of followers all around the globe.

Let us talk about some altcoins too. And the first altcoin, is Ethereum. This cryptocurrency got more attention as being one of the decentralized networks and with a platform that supported different forms of Smart Contracts. It has a network that was created and operating without any interference or control from any outsider and it is well secured against any fraudulent activity.

One of the things that made me love this digital money is, the goal behind it despite the fact that it is actually smaller when or if compared to Bitcoin (BTC)

And apart from the recent market cap which is just about $50 billion, accompanied with a promising trading price of nothing lesser than $500 per token (digitalized money appearance of Ethereum). There are just over 100.7 million ETH tokens in flowing through the network as at the year 2018 which was. Ethereum projects toward being a decentralized connected series of financial products and the easy accessibility of the whole world to them, without any restrictions such as where you are from, your belief, your position or even your tribe. But some countries are still lagging behind in the cryptocurrency development and growth, and how it can save them.

Ethereum wants to change from what we know its agreed and precise step-by-step plan was to "proof-of-stake" this year. The move is to help the cryptocurrency's network to operate with lesser energy and a highly improved swiftness of all transactions taking place in its network.

This new step-by-step plan of "proof-of-stake" is to give more room for staking ether by the users of the network, for an increment in the number of users of the network to stake their ether to the network itself.

The need for a more secured network and transaction procedures that take place in the network, has brought about the idea of changing from the initial step-by-step plan. Ethereum rewards too just Bitcoin rewards its miners with Bitcoin of more than 12 BTC, Ethereum rewards with ethers.

The second altcoin I will be adding to the list is Litecoin. Ever since it was launched in 2011 and being one of early digital money that saw Bitcoin as its guide and cautiously examined everything about Bitcoin.

And, often referred to as the "silver to Bitcoin's gold". It should not be a shocking news to know that it was created by a former Google engineer, Charlie Lee. Well, this MIT graduate, created Litecoin to run an open-source global payment network. The network is not controlled by anyone.

Litecoin is so much like Bitcoin in lot of ways, but it sure has a quicker block generation rate and that makes it provide a quicker confirmation period for a transaction.

Lots of developers accepted Litecoin from the onset but, merchants too have started accepting Litecoin too. The market cap of Litecoin from the beginning of this year is, over $12 billion and the price per token is more than $183 and it is likely, making it possible for Litecoin to be sitting comfortably as the sixth-largest digital money in the globe.

You must have heard of Bitcoin Cash (BCH). It actually takes an essential position whenever we want to talk about the history of altcoins since it was created at the early stages of altcoins and it is the most fruitful or efficacious recognizable split of the original Bitcoin.

When it comes to virtual or digital money world, what can make a split in the blockchain to happen which is always as a consequence of disputes or intense arguments between the developers and the miners of such a cryptocurrency in question.

But the only thing, is due to the decentralized characteristic of all digital money, the wholesale changes to the code that makes the token or coin implicit, at hand is or must be created as a result general consensus on it; the actual mechanism for such a process varies in a way, depending on the particular cryptocurrency in question.

My mother used to say "whenever good heads are too many in a place, expect disagreement". Having different groups and not being able to have a conclusion that has the entity of agreement embedded in it, leads to the split of digital money. Though, the original chain is retaining its originality because of the fact that, its original codes does not change. Neither, does it stop the split from actualizing its existence as a new cryptocurrency with modified codes.

This was the case for Bitcoin Cash (BCH) when it was launched in 2017. The dispute that led to its creation was making it building on the capability of greatly increasing in size. Bitcoin Cash (BCH) has an increase of block size one megabyte to eight megabytes, and still having the motive of exhibiting larger blocks to allow increased number of transactions within the blocks of the digital money and thereby having an instant effect on the swiftness of transactions. Some other changes made to the code, was the removal of Segregated Witness protocol. The market cap of Bitcoin Cash (BCH) is over $9 billion and just one token of Bitcoin Cash (BCH) is over $500 and with a circulation number placed at 18 Million plus.

I want to bring in another altcoin on board. The one that is actually getting the people's attention and has got people talking. Ladies and gentlemen reading my book with love, join me as I welcome the hyped cryptocurrency, the digital or virtual money called Ripple (XRP). It is here with us, having a market capitalization of over $ 25 billion, despite the fact that just one Ripple's (XRP) token cost 55 cents. It has a very large number of its token flowing through the network. You want a number?

My research has gotten the number for to be Over 50 billion as Ripple (XRP) is still planning to be releasing nothing more than 1 billion XRP tokens on a monthly basis, and this is going to be under the control of an in-built smart contract. And the used XRP tokens will be returned to an escrow account.

This procedure is mainly to not give even a slight chance of misuse because of its massive availability and it is definitely going to take a lot of years before the massive availability of XRP tokens can happen.

I know I have mentioned "smart contract" twice now. A smart contract means, a digital program or a transaction guideline which is basically intended to instinctively carry out, dictate or convey legally connected happenings and activities in accordance to the formulated terms of such a contract or concordance.

Another thing about Ripple that is so uniquely added to its network, is a well spread consensus mechanism through all the network of servers in its path in order to check or prove the validity of all transactions.

This kind of approach of Ripple's (XRP) network has made it practically possible for an immediate acknowledgement without any form of central authorization of anything happening in the network. This has helped the network remain decentralized, swift and pretty reliable than many other altcoins.

There is another cryptocurrency that is also influencing the market and has a very impressive trading volume. It is a utility digital money that runs as a method of payment any fees related or associated with trading on its exchange. Binance Coin (BNB) is the altcoin I am talking about right now, many use the token to make various payments on the exchange and they get discount on their trade by doing so.

Binance Coin (BNB) has its blockchain for itself and it serves as very good ground for Binance's exchange runs on too in a very decentralized manner. The exchange that

Changpeng Zhao founded is now one of the most globally accepted exchanges that is, when we are talking about trading volumes.

Binance Coin (BNB) did not run on its own decentralized blockchain before, it used to be ERC-20. It used to be a token running on another cryptocurrency blockchain that is, Ethereum's decentralized blockchain. Until the time it now had its own decentralized blockchain. It began to run on a consensus model of proof-of-stake. This year, 2021, has been a very good year for this token. It has a market capitalization of over $40 billion and just one Binance Coin (BNB) token is sold for $244.26

We are still talking about the top cryptocurrencies now. Remember to never forget that cryptocurrencies are always going to be falling and rising and vice versa. And more altcoins will still be created for investors. Having said that, let us continue with our top cryptocurrency list.

StableCoins = US Dollar$

Tether is another altcoin that has gotten the attention of the masses. It is referred to as one of the group of cryptocurrencies referred to as stable coins. Tether happens to be one of earliest and the one with much fame of that group.

Whenever a cryptocurrency is created in such a way that it has a goal to fixing a degree on its value in the digital market, to a currency or any other external measurement one can compare to in order to subdue volatility. You cannot judge these cryptocurrencies because even, the major cryptocurrencies let us say Bitcoin for instance, have had such a scenario of unpleasant volatility repetitively.

Tether as a cryptocurrency and an altcoin, and also being one of and the most popular of the stable coins, alongside with other stable coins, have an aim to make it possible to filter off wavering in price in order to catch the attention of users and giving the feeling of assurance to users who may very or a little tentative in their minds about the network of such a cryptocurrency.

Tether is fixed to the price of US dollar. Having this directly fixed price, the system makes it so much easy to make any transfer from any sort of cryptocurrency back to US dollars in an advantageous time, then going to convert to a normal or paper currency.

I will be concluding this part with just one more altcoin. You might be too familiar with other big names but, this altcoin too is not lesser either. It is an open blockchain network developed just to give possible or attainable enterprise solutions by linking financial institutions with the intention of making or having a target of mass transactions.

Stellar is the cryptocurrency that is aimed at making mass

transactions like the kinds of transaction that takes place between banks and other investment firms for instance, that undoubtedly takes many days, many intermediaries and still costing you a money, so convenient and with Stellar, it could be done almost in a forthwith manner and still costing little or even nothing at all to make your transaction.

Stellar has made a place for itself as an enterprise blockchain basically for institutions for transactions and yet, it is retaining its design as being an open blockchain open to everyone and anywhere.

I said anywhere because Stellar's system supports cross-border transactions no matter the currency. It has its own money and it is called Lumens (XLM). Its users are all required to have it so as to do all the necessary transactions they want to have on the network.

The cryptographer that created Stellar is Jed McCaleb, he was also one of the

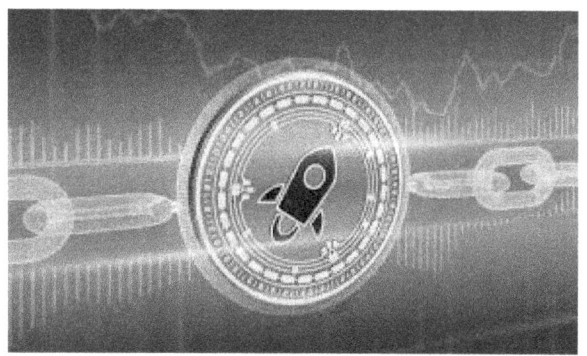

Stellar Lumens

founding members of Ripple Labs and of course, he is responsible for the development the Ripple protocol before he left his role there and co-founded Stellar Development Foundation.

I can say the risk he took paid off, Stellar native money, Lumens have more than $9 billion market capitalization and it has its price estimated at $0.40 by CoinMarketCap.

The major things that add to the popularity of cryptocurrencies are as follows:

•If the price is high even though it be wavering like Bitcoin for example.

•If the market capitalization is high

•The number of companies or industries that are accepting it

•How easy to use the cryptocurrency is

•The number of strong investors that are following it.

If you are finding it hard to calculate or to know what step to take in getting the market capitalization of any cryptocurrency at all, times what you have as the recent or current supply if the cryptocurrency by what the price is at the moment.

Once the circulating supply of the cryptocurrency is known, you can easily conclude if it is a cryptocurrency that is risky to invest in or not.

Another tip before I move to the next content, I have for you. Once you observe a very high market capitalization, it is an indication of a lesser risk because there will be more users.

CHAPTER 4; Bitcoin as the No.1 coin

What you need to get Bitcoin / How the Whales & Elon Musk played significant role in its development in the crypto market today

No one can actually say that Bitcoin (BTC) is not the major focus of many people. We cannot take the position this cryptocurrency holds away from it. It is so impossible to even sit it on the bench.

In the past few months, we have seen the way Bitcoin (BTC) has skyrocketed from the price it used to be at the beginning of last year. And, it has changed many lives just within that space of time.

The sudden and rapid increment in the value of this

cryptocurrency, did not just happen like a magic as some see it to be. It happened as a result of the high market capitalization that notable investors have considered and more are still considering, and this has made them to invest heavily in the cryptocurrency.

Now you know that Bitcoin has the highest market capitalization and a very high trading volume. Bitcoin did not get everything overnight. It started its journey in 2009 after it was mined for the first time, making it the first of all cryptocurrencies and a pace setter for other cryptocurrencies to follow. It became a standard for altcoins and became a way of life for some people. If you are not talking Bitcoin, you have not yet spoken about any cryptocurrency.

Furthermore, the market capitalization of Bitcoin being very high, makes it to be seen more as a better and obvious choice by prominent investors than any other cryptocurrencies existing out there.

Let us talk about one of the prominent investors that is following Bitcoin (BTC). The man whose company, Tesla, bought $1.5 billion worth of Bitcoin (BTC) and plans to make it possible to pay for cars bought from his company. Elon Reeve Musk, the richest man on the planet Earth right now. Elon Reeve Musk is a citizen of three countries which are South Africa, Canada and United States.

Elon Reeve Musk is an entrepreneur, industrial designer and an engineer. He founded, and he is the, CEO, CTO, and the chief designer of SpaceX. He is also the CEO, and the product architect of Tesla, Inc. Another company he founded is The Boring Company and a co-founder of Neuralink. And he was the initial co-chairman of OpenAI.

Elon Reeve Musk has a net worth of $169.8 billion (As of 20th March 2021). Elon Reeve Musk, has been talking about cryptocurrencies.

He was more focused on Dogecoin. But he has been seen talking about Bitcoin and he has even updated his bio on Twitter. Elon Reeve Musk is a man with 44.7 million followers on his social media account. He has openly spoken about Bitcoin and has given a very good remark on the cryptocurrency as he agreed to have desired to buy it a long time ago too.

The pandemic really caused a global decline on the economy of the world. Some countries that did not see the value or essence of the decentralized digital money, started seeing it and accepting it just to find a way to decrease the level at which they rely on the failing financial system.

Many economists started raising questions and we saw countries like China and even South Africa accepting cryptocurrency practically for everything and anywhere you are in the country and some started building Automated Teller Machines that could only that is built on the blockchain of cryptocurrencies.

Many investors have been shifting what they used to focus on to thinking crypto. Many investors have diversified into acquiring more and more digital assets as a way to reduce the risk of losing badly to the challenges that are surfacing.

So many people have actually criticized and spoken down on the cryptocurrency (Bitcoin). There are some billionaires that doubted the viability of Bitcoin (BTC) and some even said "it has no value". As at 2020, Bitcoin was still criticized. I am not ready to cite names of such people. So, if you are waiting for that, I am deeply sorry because I will have to disappoint you there.

But, if you are waiting to know what changed these rich investors' mind to now seeing that there is a saving grace embedded in the decentralized blockchain of the cryptocurrency (Bitcoin), then I will not disappoint not even a bit.

The decline in the financial economy and the alarming debts that has sporadically

However, as debt and money supplies continue to rise steadily, Bitcoin's potential as a viable alternative to the current system and a way to hedge against expansionist monetary policies is rapidly being recognized.

What can I say?

You should expect people to be influenced especially when the influencer is an icon like Elon Reeve Musk. Just a word and step from him has really added to the market capitalization of Bitcoin (BTC). Elon Reeve Musk is a big influencer, and has gotten to a level that he can influence any asset's value with just his action or word.

It is not a new thing anymore as same thing happened with Signal and GameStop to mention a few. So, the shocking thing is, Elon Reeve Musk just increased the value of Bitcoin with just a tweet about it alone.

There are individual investors, deciding on Bitcoin (BTC) and if it is going to be a short-term rise in value for the cryptocurrency (Bitcoin). Ordinarily, seeing people buying a digital asset will also trigger your curiosity. This is what happens with smart investors, they will buy and continue to buy assets that others will not find wasteful or useless to buy.

Elon Reeve Musk is a tech billionaire and a very strong personality. Just changing his bio to #bitcoin made an increase in the value of the cryptocurrency by 20%. He admitted regretting not buying it earlier but now buying it after.

With Elon Reeve Musk being one of the big investors following Bitcoin (BTC), many more are going to join as the week has not yet ended. The presence of Elon Reeve Musk has pushed the value of the cryptocurrency higher and it is getting higher and higher even with its market capitalization and with this, its value has a potential of hitting even $100 thousand and above.

If an entrepreneur invests in an asset, it is a diversification technique. The price of the cryptocurrency, Bitcoin (BTC) skyrocketed to up to 67% as at the first of this year, 2021. Elon Reeve Musk surely knows that this is a sign of good return on the $1.5 billion that the company invested in the cryptocurrency, Bitcoin (BTC).

People are forgetting that Tesla will not actually be the first company to go into Bitcoin investment or even adding it to its balance sheet. Where will you put a company like MicroStrategy?

You may be saying "it is a software company but Tesla is not" or you want to say that "the money Tesla has invested in this cryptocurrency, Bitcoin (BTC) is way too much than the $250 million worth of Bitcoin (BTC) that MicroStrategy bought in August" but, do not neglect the fact that, what that company (MicroStrategy) bought at that price now has a very solid value of about $3.1 billion. An entrepreneur will always look before investing in anything at all.

There is no doubt that the cryptocurrency, Bitcoin (BTC), is created as high-powered computer race against other electronic machines to find values of intricate mathematical riddles.

The intensity of the energy process making it on so much reliance on fossil fuels, especially coal which is termed dirty and what I am talking about in short is Bitcoin (BTC) mining. This is the major critic that Tesla's CEO is getting as Tesla is green.

Now, let us talk about how the whales of Bitcoin (BTC) have impacted also on the value of the cryptocurrency, Bitcoin (BTC). First of all, whatever or whoever is called a Bitcoin whale, is a MicroStrategy person or an entity that has got a lot of the cryptocurrency, Bitcoin sitting in the digital wallet of such a person (BTC). You should know that 40% of the total market of Bitcoin is owned by just 1000 people according to Investopedia.

Those whales have the capability to manipulate the cryptocurrency valuations. The big whales can easily push the price of the cryptocurrency, Bitcoin (BTC). At any given time that these people make just a trade each, it almost instantly causing a high degree of change in the price of Bitcoin, and this people's investment is actually very intimidating to smaller people investing in the cryptocurrency too.

"The big players can easily move the price" because the bitcoin trading market is very thin. Anyone of them could crash it" said by Telegraph report.

"Whales can be a problem for Bitcoin because the concentration of wealth, particularly if it sits unmoved in an account and lowers liquidity, which, in turn, can increase price volatility. Volatility is further increased if the whale moves a large quantity of bitcoin at once. If the seller is trying to sell bitcoin for state currency, the lack of liquidity and large transaction size could put downward pressure on the price of bitcoin, as other market participants see the transaction and also try to sell, creating a fire sale" said by Investopedia.

Bitcoin's (BTC) all users' names are made anonymous, but only the ledger, displays the whole of the address and transaction. Making it possible, for us to actually guess to a degree of certainty about who these Bitcoin whales' identities can be.

You should know that if we are going to start guessing who these Bitcoin whales' identities could be, we should look firstly at the cryptographer that actually created the cryptocurrency, Bitcoin (BTC) in 2009.

Satoshi Nakamoto, the Bitcoin (BTC) mystery cryptographer. The puzzle has not been wholly solved until recently, something unfolded.

The likely guess of who Satoshi Nakamoto could really be is an Australian businessman.

There is a claim that this man actually created the

cryptocurrency, Bitcoin (BTC). Craig Wright, is believed to have done so with the help he got from his friend, Dave Kleiman.

Craig Wright was sued in 2019 by his friend. It was reported that this affected half of the a million and hundred thousand BTC he had.

No one knows for sure if this is actually a genuine information as everything surrounding it is secretly done and it seems so complex to fathom. But, if Craig Wright have that much, then he is a big whale.

Another Bitcoin whale I will put on the list are the Winklevoss (Cameron and Tyler). The twins got into the game early enough to talk about it and to have over 100,000 Bitcoin (BTC).

Another big whale on my Bitcoin whale's list is Barry Silbert. The CEO and the founder of Digital Currency Group. He has over 75 bitcoin-related companies around. He owns CoinDesk. CoinDesk is a notable source of Bitcoin news.

At the rate at which Bitcoin (BTC) is being accepted around the globe, and many more investors are anxious to invest in the cryptocurrency, Bitcoin (BTC) it is said to be doubling in its market capitalization in the space few weeks despite its volatility.

CHAPTER 5; Ethereum as No.2 coin

Ethereum today / Ethereum 2.0 - A game-changer / it's effect on Miners

Sweet joy and happiness are what I feel anytime I get to talk about certain altcoins such as this particular one for instance.

Knowing fully well that it is an altcoin that is really moving fast and found its way up the ladder to be in a serious competitive position, I love it.

What can I say about this beauty that will be enough for you to consent into the investment of cryptocurrencies especially this beauty?

How about a little bit revision? Ethereum is a cryptocurrency (altcoin) that has got more attention as being one of the decentralized network and with a platform that supported different forms of Smart Contracts that got more attention during the pandemic and lot of people used these Smart Contracts to gather lots of this cryptocurrency. Forsage, Million Money and Lion Share just to mention a few, are parts of Smart Contracts built on the blockchain of the cryptocurrency, Ethereum. Since it has a network that was created and operating without any interference or control from any outsider and it is well secured against any fraudulent activity.

Ethereum is the second cryptocurrency after Bitcoin (BTC). And, it has a very large market capitalization.

Pretty early this month the other version of the cryptocurrency that we have been waiting for, that is the upgraded version (Ethereum 2.0) of Ethereum came to reality, there is an update already from the founder of the cryptocurrency, Vitalik Buterin. We know for sure that with Ethereum 2.0, there will be great new features, and I am already falling in love with it already even before its arrival.

You should not forget the crucial role that this cryptocurrency played, it served more as roadblock remover talking about smart contracts and it has set a fortified ground for any or many developers to make use of its platform.

Ethereum (ETH) is Ethereum 1.0, do not forget that I said that it uses proof-of-work consensus to complete all requirements or the work to be done. At least we all know that, that is the first and initial algorithm if the cryptocurrency's blockchain network.

The summary of it is, there has to be some certain participants of the blockchain.

Now that the use-to-be consensus, has been modified and it is now proof-of-stake and this is a symbol or a sign of something big enough to change the game. Proof-of-stake runs as some particular participants also referred to as validators, protect the whole betting on which of the block is going to be valid next and whoever gets the right bet will be rewarded while, those that do not get the right one, are penalized for it.

Proof-of-stake happens to be more energy efficient because it requires not make use of great computation in order to unravel the whole puzzles. Ethereum (ETH) 2.0 with its new consensus, is to arrive with so many attractiveness, as it has a more fortified or heightened security level and with its ability to change in scale or size.

It is highly projected that, with this newly modified consensus, more energy will be saved. But the thing is, miners are also the participants and validators of transactions like crypto-staking and they have been given responsibility of examining both transactions and the sum of money and the actual length of time any holder could hold their assets for which is to give them a meaningful and secured position from what seems difficult to be dislodged and an uncomely merit in the market with that much power and awareness capable enough to give a tacit suggestion into the concentrated or centralized system.

There is an argument going on that staking will not do anything good than causing a centralized effect on the network in spite of the issue that led to the saying that concerning Proof-of-work (PoW) "the larger the mining farm, the higher the return due to economies of scale".

Opposite of what had earlier been expected, with Proof-of-stake (PoS), little economies of scale are present in this consensus such that, cost of staking is to be so much similar either a person is to stake for instance 40 Ethereum (ETH) or 40,000 Ethereum (ETH).

Furthermore, the recent projection for my beauty, Ethereum (ETH) 2.0, public network should accept between 1,000 and 5,000 TPS, and you just cannot try to make any comparison of this cryptocurrency (Ethereum 2.0) modified consensus with Ethereum (ETH) 1.0 as it can at least allow 30 TPS.

Going through many people's thought on this there is one I love and cannot just wave it away. Zipmex says "it will take several years as it is highly likely that by that point, people will have already been using layer 2 solution such as rollups to address scalability issues".

There is a high increment in the consciousness and the ongoing large number of adoptions everywhere. Some of us actually believe that the price is actually being pushed by notion. But taking a critical look at things, sum of transactions and the daily gas are fixed in the green with the network usage of over 90%.

Ethereum has a feature for protecting exchange details and assets, you just have to be updated with the news of the cryptocurrency, Ethereum (ETH) as concerned with its movement and its directed change. It is always imperative and resourceful having a framework that projects into the future as the time is still very far.

2020 has made many activities or processes move online as a result of the pandemic that gave rise to staying at home and social distancing. It really hastened every form of activities that are or were frequently happening that have been digitalized to grow and develop faster including the speed of payment to become even faster and easier.

The pandemic legacy was not just death or recession, it opened up the eyes of people to new opportunities. This inconvenience we faced triggered the urge we had and many of us moved our businesses online. Same way it contributed to the advancement of the blockchain and many Smart Contracts and it gained the advancement as a result of not just the most obvious reason which is, the pandemic but, because of its decentralized nature of the network of the cryptocurrency, Ethereum (ETH) and it gave rise to its prominence.

The construction of a plan of action regarding Ethereum 2.0 has actually gave many goosebumps already. This is the future of a blockchain community. We will definitely have many surprise packages as regards to the advanced cryptocurrency, Ethereum (ETH) 2.0.

I am not a guru, in fact I put a lot of hard work into things before I can be able to say "I have got this". Neither am I some seer but, I really do think that, the steady rate of Ethereum over the past few weeks is not some miracle of

God but, because of the promising values of the cryptocurrency in the offing which is Ethereum (ETH) 2.0 that has shifted from its used-to-be Proof -of-Work (PoW) to Proof-of-Stake (PoS) consensus.

No one should take away the leading from the jungle or stop it from roaring neither can we say that the lioness being the hunter, to keep quiet or stop hunting. Bitcoin (BTC) has the highest market capitalization and value, but for an altcoin, Ethereum has done and is doing pretty well.

As an altcoin, this cryptocurrency might just be most essentially planned endeavor, with an actual goal and accomplishment in several steps or stages in the blockchain virtual world. Unarguably, the cryptocurrency, (ETH) Ethereum has second largest market capitalization in all the cryptocurrencies that we have and it is second to Bitcoin (BTC) and it is like a vessel carrying other vessels that are smaller.

What I am saying is this, Ethereum allows some other blockchain projects and applications such as Defi applications to advance. The cryptocurrency is stretching its hands wide and ready to show us its second generation and how much more it has gotten to the point of growth and development or advancement in everything its first generation has been offering to us.

What has been a concern about Ethereum (ETH) 2.0 is that, as much as it likes carrying smaller vessels on with its blockchain, the more applications get higher and higher on this blockchain, the costs get increased and there is a depletion in the level of its speed.

I remember using the abbreviation of TPS earlier, I am sorry I did not break that down. Transactions per second, that is the meaning of Post the abbreviation. And, whenever there is a congestion in the cryptocurrency's (ETH 1.0), the transaction per second has reached its limit already and there be a serious hindrance to any Ethereum (ETH) 1.0 applications' designing or programming.

When it comes to the vision behind the conception of the cryptocurrency Ethereum (ETH) 2.0, it is going to be a need to groom Ethereum (ETH) until it becomes fully capable or mature enough to take up the responsibility of assisting humanity.

In the grooming stage as it is still in, there is an essential need to make so many sensible and creative modifications to be the advancement of its characteristics such as security, ability to be sustainable and its size. For Ethereum (ETH) to be fully exploited, it needed to shift its consensus algorithm from Proof-of-Work (PoW) to Proof-of-Stake (PoS).

The plan is not even using electronic machines (computers) as nodes to a miner, it is basically the users, staking their Ethereum (ETH) to be a validator and given the kind of responsibilities the miners in the consensus algorithm of Proof-of-Work (PoW).

Miners too stake but, they are to stake 32 Ethereum (ETH) to actually become a validator. We are expecting energy efficiency on a very great level at least better than before, barriers to entry reduction, hardware required becoming way reduced and to buttress everything, better or higher immunity to any form or sign of centralization.

Ethereum (ETH) 2.0 is designed to increase its previous shard chains, which is intended to cause a significant advancement in the speed of its transaction per second (TPS).

Sharding is the kind of a careful step-by-step procedure taken with the intention of splitting a database horizontally enough to give a spreading impact on the load, as it is viewed to reduce the Ethereum's (ETH) network congestion and finally, increasing the transaction per second (TPS) by creating new chains.

There is another chain involved in this matter of Ethereum (ETH) 2.0 and that chain is referred to as "Beacon Chain" and is known as a "Phase 0" on the Ethereum's complex roadmaps, it is a fundamental part of Ethereum (ETH) 2.0.

The intended plan is for it to be a forerunner for Proof-of-Stake (Pos) to the Ethereum (ETH) system, and to take the role of a coordinator. This particular chain received state details from Shard Chains (64 shard chains) and ensuring its availability for other shard chains in the system just to ensure the complete synchronicity in the network. It also has an added responsibility of managing validators, from stake registration to issuing rewards and penalties too.

The validators, happen to be the main participants of Ethereum (ETH) 2.0, and are charged with the responsibility of keeping the network protected throughout the year and seven days a week.

The higher percentage of the whole digital programming for keeping the Ethereum (ETH) 2.0 network always online and so active pertains to the validators, the major and biggest responsibility they have is, simply to guarantee their individual internet connection is not fluctuating and all the machines they are in charge of are all very connected to a stable source of electrical power.

CHAPTPER 6; ALT coins & their performances in the crypto market

Altcoins are the "not-bitcoins" and the "I have to prove myself that I am worth the attention" kind of coins or tokens. But you must have known that already.

How much do you think life will bring to your table when you are already doubtful?

BestLife said that "Maintaining a healthy dose of curiosity about the world around you will help sharpen your mind, make you happier, strengthen your relationships, and even improve your productivity".

There are so many people who still believe that some things do not count, it does not matter to them because they are not in that line of business or something, and thereby giving "why exactly should I care?" kind of attitude to every other thing.

Your environment includes the activities that are going on online or offline too. The talks about the cryptocurrencies good enough to invest in, are part of the tiny details of all the activities in your environment.

I am not saying that, if you do not invest in a digital asset such as a cryptocurrency or even cryptocurrencies; you cannot be in a better investment. There are other things going on that you can pick from and then invest in.

But a digital asset such as a cryptocurrency, is a good investment that you can be rest assured that you are most definitely getting your high returns from it. You can actually save for your retirement, reach any financial goal you have set for yourself, support others, or even expand your business as you are earning your high returns from your Cryptocurrency investment. If you invest in not just any cryptocurrency but "the cryptocurrencies", you are absolutely not wasting your money but, you are grooming your money through "the cryptocurrencies".

Listen, I am not telling you or anybody else that it is a must to start investing in cryptocurrencies neither am I saying that if you do not invest in it you cannot reach your financial goal or have financial stability, expand your business, save towards retirement and so on. I am a preacher of paths and when I see potentials in any path, I call the people's attention to such a path. Now, it is a digital path I have seen much potentials that will be even more as we proceed more into the year.

I know that there is a saying in the Bible that "do not join multitude" but sometimes, multitudes are the ones to bring you into what can help you stand financially. Whenever you see the multitude going one way pay attention first and critically observe that way or place, they are going and let the Spirit tell you if the multitude going that way is a sign or not. I know one thing for sure, you cannot see people running and you will not become suddenly cautious of the situation at hand that will surely make you ask that "what is going on?"

I speak not against anything; I have to clear the air on that again. It is a very sensitive period to not care about the people's beliefs. I meant not even the slightest disregard or disrespect.

Having said all that, I will make a list of the cryptocurrencies that worth your investments. In addition to this, from an economist angle or view, an investment happens whenever a purchase of goods that are not consumed today but are used in the future to generate wealth, then that is said to be an investment. But, whenever a loss is encountered, then people tend to call or term or tag it a bad investment.

So, what about its meaning when it comes to finance?

Investment is a financial asset bought with the idea that the asset will provide income further or will later be sold at a higher cost price for a profit.

Without no further talks on it, the things or something that can give or make the future productive in the economy, is the summary of it all.

Investment does not just come into play for man, it came as a result of man's desire to be successful in life. He needs to grow his wealth and also having an additional income.

He knows that the only way out is to invest, so as to protect and adding more to his present and future long-term financial security. You should have it in mind that any money generated or gotten from your investments, if managed well can guarantee you a financial security and income.

Now I am suggesting a place you can actually put your money and get your high returns as an investor. The high market capitalization alone should give you a sense of confidence.

In an attempt to help you know the particular digital assets (cryptocurrency) that are so sure to make you have the kind of income you want to be getting, I have put it upon myself to help you know them and you can then decide to go with anyone or two or more of them.

I want you to know that at this particular junction, I am only talking about the top altcoins that you can put your money in.

And, I have explained the meaning of an altcoin but if by now you do not know where the altcoins value stand, I will tell you that where they stand is where we are going to pick our favorites from as per the market capitalization and trading volume.

It is either you want to invest in it or you want to trade with it either way, you will be in the system and the game already started from there. The goal is to do either of the two to increase what you put in it.

The altcoins are doing pretty well in the market but you know things will always be better than another one. Same goes for these digital assets too, as some are performing far too well than the others.

It is now based on how to tell which particular ones will be outstanding and really

Ascertaining which ones will outperform the markets is where fundamental analysis comes into play. Projects with a strong chance of gaining user adoption and lasting the long-term offer some of the best chances of healthy returns.

Without wasting time anymore, let us go into the list of the altcoins that have placed themselves in at the top, and have gained lot of attention from people all around the world.

Ethereum (ETH)

The first on the list as per the market capitalization is Ethereum (ETH). I know that this particular cryptocurrency, Ethereum (ETH) has been really pronounced in this volume, it is the cryptocurrency that is getting much attention around the globe. The native currency of Ethereum (ETH) is Ether and it is the cryptocurrency designed to be on top of the open source, Ethereum blockchain, and it used in running smart contracts.

This is the kind of cryptocurrency that acts more as an energizer and allows all the smart contracts to run smoothly. Ether is not capped in its supply, and that supply that I said is not capped is actually true but it has a scheduled supply, it is mostly said to be a minimum and yet, necessary to secure the network. It is decided on by members of Ethereum's (ETH) community.

Many of the decentralized applications are actually built on Ethereum (ETH) and the digital money accounts also for the highest percentage of the overall funds staked in the DeFi projects.

Told you already about the modification of the version of Ethereum (ETH) 2.0 the future cryptocurrency, with it there will be a rapid fee reduction and multiple new DApps getting a chance to illuminate.

If you are joining this train, then try not to forget to have your ticket close (Ether). Ether is seriously becoming more resourceful nowadays.

Chainlink

Another altcoin that is featuring on this list is definitely going to be a cryptocurrency called Chainlink (LINK) Chainlink is a tokenized oracle network, it is the kind of cryptocurrency that gives price and events details collected from on-chain and real-world sources.

This is the cryptocurrency that was created in 2017 by Sergey Nazarov. Basically, it was designed to proffer a solution to the "oracle problem" or the capability to get the off-chain data or the details needed to run many blockchain-based smart contracts.

The token does act or function to motivate participants to not just provide, but to use this data.

Something interesting about this cryptocurrency is, it actually does not have or own its own blockchain. What it does is, it lets its token protocol which is blockchain of a software component and can run on so many different blockchains at the same time. It has a market capitalization of more than $23 billion. While the price per token is $33

Polkadot

Polkadot (DOT) is the most important one out of all the successfully executed projects by Web3 Foundation, carefully designed to link all private and consortium chains, general and the kinds of networks that does not need authorization, oracles, and to-come technologies that are time ahead for their creation.

The cryptocurrency is an internet facilitator that is, a digital place for independent blockchains to be able to carry-out all exchange details and transactions in an untrusting manner through the Polkadot relay chain.

It has the kind of unique aims that it can make it so much easy to logically create and link all the decentralized applications, services, and institutions. It has a price of $32 and its market capitalization is more than $13 billion.

Litecoin (LTC)

This particular cryptocurrency (altcoin) was launched late 2011 by Charlie Lee Litecoin is a cryptocurrency launched in late 2011 by former Google and Coinbase engineer Charlie Lee.

Charlie Lee had to emulate the codebase of Bitcoin (BTC) in order for him to actualize his dream, and he made it and added his own touch which led to increasing the whole number of supply, and making an increment to the speed at which the new blocks are imputed into the blockchain.

To be candid, Charlie Lee did a very good job on this cryptocurrency (altcoin), and he even quadrupled the number of Bitcoin (BTC) there is and gave it to

Litecoin (LTC).

What I am saying is that there is approximately 84 million LTC and that is the number that it can be forever created, it cannot go below the quadrupled total supply of Bitcoin (BTC). An added detail is, this altcoin can also create new blocks every 2.5 minutes too, which is four times faster than Bitcoin (BTC).

Stellar (XLM)

Stellar (XLM) is a cryptocurrency (altcoin) and it is not a news to you anymore that its native currency is Lumen. Stellar (XLM) is an open source blockchain payment system.

We have gone through its purpose already but we can go through it briefly. Stellar has a goal to link financial institutions through the blockchain and proffering a so-cheap kind of transactions in the developing markets.

Stellar operates with an agreement algorithm instead of what is called "traditional mining network" to confirm transactions.

It is like that because when it comes to the transferring of

Lumens, it does not need to seek any form of approval from any traditional cryptocurrency miner, the Stellar has the kind of network that enables quicker transactions than many other blockchain-based systems.

Ripple (XRP)

Some of the cryptocurrencies (altcoins) that will make you smile intoxicatingly, one of them is Ripple (XRP). Ripple (XRP) is the type of cryptocurrency (altcoin) referred to as a "Real Time Gross Settlement System" and it is undoubtedly a money exchange and it has got the network that supports payment to a remote recipient. It is designed in such a way that its independent servers validate.

The digital money that is traded here is named as XRP and all the transfer times are at an instance. Without any tension, Ripple (XRP) can be easily exchanged very often for most other currencies with its greatly outstanding selling discourse being the shunning of fees and wait times commonly associated with banks especially.

The thing is, it is not even made up of a blockchain, instead, it is a Hash Tree and neither can its currency be mined because, there is a specific number of coins 100 billion.

Something that seems so unlike most of the cryptocurrencies is that, other cryptocurrencies (altcoins) always have a focus on escaping banking institutions, instead of that, Ripple (XRP) is prominent enough to be in touch with banks and so much wants to be part of their family by partnering with them. It has a market capitalization worth more than $25 billion. As for price per XRP is concerned, you are only spending just cents and it has a fixed circulation supply set at 39 billion.

EOS (EOS)

You rarely see many people talking about some cryptocurrencies (altcoins) and the rest for this is, some people just do not want to get themselves involved in any other cryptocurrencies (altcoins) that they just focus on one only.

Another good altcoin is EOS. This is the type of cryptocurrency that has its native digital money to still be EOS.IO blockchain foundation with a smart contract distinct capability.

EOS (EOS) cryptocurrency can trace its origin back to the company named Block.one, since they created EOS.IO in the month of September of the year 2017, and it turned out to be so much of a success that it now has pretty more than

100 decentralized applications or DApps with thousands of everyday active users.

It so much helps in actualizing the existence of DApps through their digital creation by software developers. The platform is more scalable than so many other blockchain networks, with no so much of the ability to process one million transactions per second (TPS) with no fees. It has a price $5 and a market capitalization of more than $2 billion.

Bitcoin Cash (BCH)

I have talked about this cryptocurrency before as it came to be as a result of the splitting-up of an existing process into itself and a child process executing parts of the same program.

You understand that it is as a result of this that brought about this cryptocurrency. Bitcoin Cash (BCH)

Bitcoin cash (BCH) as a digital money, has a total market capitalization sum up of more than $14 billion, a digital market price of $505 as per coin. It has its overall number of supply of about 17.2 million Bitcoin Cash (BTC).

Tether (USDT)

Tether is another altcoin that has found its way right into the heart of people and it is one of the most traded cryptocurrencies at the moment. Tether (USDT). Oftentimes, it is referred to as USDT. This cryptocurrency has a balanced currency that is very redeemable for a dollar. In summary of it all, let us say you keep $50 USDT, you can easily exchange it for $50.

It was founded in 2014 and right from its Genesis, Tether has gotten quite large number of attention and popularity because of its unparalleled characteristics. Looking critically at the record of Tether, it is so evident that the cryptocurrency has always been on the favorite list of people in cryptocurrency.

What most traders do is, use the altcoin to actually replace their dollar. Since it is so easy and very fast to exchange it either it is between you and your friends or partners or on exchanges. Rather than, transacting and transferring all around through the bank you are using.

Tether is as easy as a piece of cake when it comes to purchasing and selling, it is so available whenever you are ready and wherever you are, it is right there at your location and you can easily get your cryptocurrency.

Most of the followers and users especially the traders of Tether, commonly make use of it as a safe means to keep funds on markets when traders worry about the stock, especially in a highly risky condition.

Tether is an altcoin (cryptocurrency) and the most popular of the stablecoins, and it the digital money that is based on a blockchain and whose digital currency in circulation is backed with a virtually equal amount to traditional currencies, like the Japanese Yen, Euro, or Dollars, which can be either deposited or transferred the account created in anyone of the designated banks around.

We are looking up to this cryptocurrency to become the best way to preserve gains from the world of the virtual currency. But the gospel truth is, Tether's future absolutely depends on the to-come of cryptocurrency too. There are so many distinct rules and regulations that are targeted at cryptocurrency across the globe.

Do not see it as a news right now, $33 million Tether has been rendered immobile as a consequential result of KuCoin hack, and with such a move I must say that, it is crystal clear Tether as a cryptocurrency retains a very formidable centralized digital asset that rejects the decentralization of the blockchain ecosystem. That said, it's still the most trusted and oldest stable coin in the crypto virtual ecosystem.

The overall number of its circulation supply sum up is more than $19 billion. Tether is the largest and oldest of the stablecoins, the group referred to as "stablecoins" has more than 40 stable coins trading, and many of them are linked to different sovereign currencies or gold, silver, and unique drawing rights (SDR) for instance.

CHAPTER 7: Decentraland (Mana) a promising ALT coin - How ATARI games are being built on this platform.

Decentraland is actually an (altcoin) (cryptocurrency) that was created to have a virtual reality blockchain platform of based on another altcoin which happens to be Ethereum (ETH), making it easy for its users to buy, groom and even monetize applications.

This cryptocurrency is called Decentraland, happens to be a 3D world that its users put two tokens into use to make it possible to interact with the platform, and buy things such as land, goods and services "in-world."

It surely is, a cryptocurrency of two division, which is means a limited sum of the parcels referred to as LAND (non-fungible ERC721 token simulates its appearance), and whenever you as a user want it, you can purchase it smoothly with MANA, which is an ERC20 token.

Having LAND as a possession, does give users a full ownership privilege, which means that they get to have a complete control over the environment, and applications they designed within their land making use of Decentraland as a foundation.

Decentraland as an alternative cryptocurrency (altcoin), successfully finished its original coin offering precisely, month of August of 2017 and, realized close to $24 million worth of Ethereum (ETH), Bitcoin (BTC), and other altcoins (cryptocurrencies).

The onset supply of MANA was distributed in a way such as the following: 40% initial sale which was sold, 20% distribution of it to the community and its partners (these are, stipends that facilitated an instant communication with Decentraland) 20% of it was also given to the founding team, and lastly, 20% of it was held back by the Decentraland foundation.

The users from the onset, bought LAND in two distinct auctions, the first one of it, took place in December 2017 to be precise, while the second of it, took place in the last of month of the year 2018.

Every single one of the auctions was conducted strictly as a "Dutch auction," which in a simple sentence is, each one of the available parcels was set at a very similar starting price and decreased as the auction proceeded until, it got to a very soothing price for a user.

As shocking it may sound it is true that anytime LAND was bought, the MANA digital money or currency (cryptocurrency) that was used for the transaction was burned, not like it was literally burned but such a token will be immediately deleted or transferred to a void or irrecoverable address.

As the secondary market is concerned, the transactions such as "purchase" and "sale" of LAND takes place only on the decision or wise choices made by the primary owner of LAND parcels.

With everything that have been explained, it can be deduced without stress that Decentraland is a virtual or digital reality platform powered by or running on the Ethereum (ETH) blockchain and it is in such a way that it uses two tokens.

A MANA is an ERC-20 token that has a multi-purpose characteristic, remember it is without any further questions burned just to be able to claim LAND (it is an ERC-721 token), and also used to make in-world purchases of goods and services.

Decentraland is logically divided into a total sum of 90,000 parcels of LAND, and each of them measuring 16 x 16 "meters."

In addition to this, a MANA can be stored in ERC-20 compatible wallets without having any stress or any critical things that can be a puzzle.

The total number supply of MANA is strictly put or fixed

at nothing more than 2,644,403,343 MANA.

Changes or modification to or of parcels of LAND are always registered in the Ethereum (ETH) LAND smart contract and then confirmed by the Ethereum (ETH) blockchain.

Having said that, Atari, is the gaming company behind the notable games such as Pacman, Asteroids and Pong,

now intends to actually develop an altcoin (cryptocurrency) casino by partnering with Decentral Games.

A press release shared with CoinDesk that, Atari-branded casino will be built in "Vegas City," and of course, it is going to be a massive gaming district in partnership with Decentraland metaverse an Ethereum-based do not neglect it because that is the foundation of Decentraland cryptocurrency. This gaming district will be as an initial lease of two years.

What to expect?

A virtual or digital world that allows all players take

absolute control of any avatar's body as they are interacting with the virtual or digital world or better still, "metaverse." Atari knows how to spot a good business and that is so strategic.

Decentral Games, is a part or a component of the Decentraland ecosystem, it does seem to be the first of its kind as a community-owned metaverse crypto casino.

This new casino, based on Decentral Games' technology, will have Atari-themed games and with that I meant it will not be without the Atari Special game based on skill rather than luck as it is a new wave for them and it should be more technically sound.

The Players also will be able to earn for themselves the Decentral Games' traditional token which is $DG playing with MANA (+6.23%), DAI (+0.05%) and Atari tokens.

All the token holders of $DG will find it possible to also be able to put them into use in order to participate in governance and company-related decision making, according to the release.

CoinMarketCap puts its Decentraland price per token at $0.91 and its trading volume of more than $2 million.

CHAPTER 8: Miners & their effects on prices and coins.

All the existing cryptocurrencies were created and are commonly protected through the cryptographic algorithms that are maintained and verified in a process or procedure referred to as mining.

It involves having a network of electronic machines (computers) or making use of specialized hardware such as application-specific integrated circuits (ASICs) process and authenticate the transactions. The process motivates the people (miners) who are running the network with the cryptocurrency.

There are actually many cryptocurrencies but it is just some of them that are basically or readily traded by anyone in the globe using the digital or virtual money and the other thing is that too many of the not so notable have market capitalization that is far too less than what you can imagine.

How about using the pioneer of all the cryptocurrencies that are known to man right now as an illustration?

Bitcoin (BTC) for example, was created by the mysterious Satoshi Nakamoto and was publicly released in 2009 as open-source code.

The technology of blockchain made it so that all actually work, providing a systematically structured data which is referred to as "blocks" are broadcasted, authenticated, and entered in a public, well spread database through a network of communication endpoints called nodes.

Even though Bitcoin (BTC) happens to be the king and it is obviously the most famous of all the cryptocurrencies, it still did not stop even in the alternative coins not to have their own most notables and the ones with a very attractive characteristic from coming into the picture either. For instance, the second and most sought out cryptocurrency in the altcoins, Ethereum (ETH) really took what we know as "smart contracts" up a notch just by making the programming languages required to code them even more reachable for the developers.

There has to be a meeting of the minds, or having conditional transactions, are written as code and ran and this is as long as all demands are absolutely met) in Ethereum's (ETH) blockchain.

Ethereum (ETH), furthermore, has earned

an infamy as a result of the fact that a hacker took advantage of the loophole or weakness which was detectable and could give room for an attack to reduce system's security in the Digital Autonomous Organization (DAO) running on Ethereum's (ETH) software, and thereby

"have one's hand in the till" kind of situation as the hacker went away with $50 million worth of Ether which is the native currency of Ethereum (ETH). This occurrence, gave rise to the development of Ethereum Classic, based the original blockchain, and Ethereum, its upgraded version of Ethereum (ETH) 2.0.

There are some other popular cryptocurrencies such as: Litecoin, Dogecoin, Monero.

Litecoin is basically a technical improvement of Bitcoin and it is so capable of the realization of faster turnarounds with the aid of its Scrypt mining algorithm while Bitcoin uses SHA-256.

The Litecoin (LTC) network is very able to produce 84 million Litecoin (LTC) and that is four times as many cryptocurrency units approves by Bitcoin (BTC).

Monero is another popular cryptocurrency that is so known for its use of ring signatures, which is a kind of a digital signature and its CryptoNote application layer protocol which is designed to secure the privacy of its transactions which entails the amount, origin, and destination as well.

Some cryptocurrencies such as Dogecoin are not the much-hyped type of cryptocurrency probably because of the reason behind its original development or designed, which was for educational or entertainment purposes, and it was intended for a more detailed demographic. Which is going to be very capable of producing uncapped Dogecoins, it also utilizes Scrypt to drive the currency along.

All these digital or virtual assets called cryptocurrencies, have no restrictions because anyone can transfer them anytime, from anywhere, without any form of delay or some sort of any additional/hidden charges from anyone or anything standing as an intermediary.

With their noticeable characteristics, they are actually more protected from all sorts of fraud and even identity theft as these cryptocurrencies cannot be made counterfeit from, and all the personal or discreet details are behind a fortified cryptographic wall.

As great as it sounds, it is rather unfortunate, that the same apparent profitability, convenience, and how much or the degree or level at which the details are hidden behind pseudonym, it has also made the cryptocurrencies so ideal for cyber-criminals, this was showed by ransomware operators.

As the fame of these cryptocurrencies increase occurring at the same time with the occurrences of malware that can infect systems and devices, turning them into a legion of cryptocurrency-mining machines.

Cryptocurrency mining, for any miner, involves a computationally thorough execution demanding for meaningful resources from the dedicated processors, graphics cards, and other hardware.

While mining does give money, but there are just so many warnings involved in it. Even the profit is dependent on the miner's investment on hardware and so forth, we have not even mentioned the electricity costs to power all hardware's purchased and every other electronic device too.

Another thing is that, cryptocurrencies are mined in blocks; in Bitcoin (BTC), as an example, for every time a specific number of hashes are answered, the number of Bitcoins (BTC) that can be possibly awarded to that miner per block will be divide into halve.

We should know that the Bitcoin (BTC) network is actually developed to produce the cryptocurrency at every 10 minutes, the complexity of solving another hash has to be adjusted.

If increment starts showing in the mining power, then the demand for a resource to be able to mine a new block pile up right there and gradually. The payouts are to an extent rather a little or too small and

at a given period of time, it starts decrease eventually.

Because of this particular reason, some miners turn to using malware to play around these unfavorable factors. They become cyber-criminal miners.

Some internet-linked devices and machines, are quite fast enough to process a network data, but do not have the wide capacity for number-crunching.

To offset this, cryptocurrency-mining malware are designed to zombify botnets of computers to perform these tasks. Others avoided subtlety altogether-in 2014, Harvard's supercomputer cluster Odyssey was used to illicitly mine dogecoins.

Pardon me for bringing in all of that, how about we talk solely about the content of concern?

For many years now, Bitcoin (BTC) miners have already cut back on the energy implications by simply moving their production to China.

China happens to be a country that has been said to account for 60% of Bitcoin (BTC) production operations.

And, large number of the Chinese Bitcoin (BTC) mines are located right in its Sichuan province, and place is said to be where hydropower dominates.

Iceland, is the type that has the resource to produce a natural cooling Arctic air for any overheated systems and it also uses geothermal energy (heat under the ground used to heat water and make really steamed to turn generator turbines and get electricity from it as an end product).

It is also, a very prominent location for Bitcoin (BTC) mining operations. Even though the Chinese miners have not given an estimate yet, in relative to Bitcoin (BTC) production costs implications.

But Genesis mining, that moved its mines from China to Iceland, has now been able to make an estimation of $60 for the company so as to be able to produce a single Bitcoin (BTC).

The estimated cost of production model for Bitcoin (BTC) of which we know that energy is the main cost, can make anyone conclude that technological advancement in the form of a faster and more energy-efficient hardware's, will bring down the digital market price of Bitcoin (BTC). Since mining is not just a process you just embark on like that and if things become easier, it could bring down the price of the cryptocurrency.

There are new developments to actually notice in things as a real-world mining efficiency increases, it is probably as a result of competition in business, the break-even price for Bitcoin (BTC) producers will tend to decrease as the low-cost producers are willingly going to keep competing in the market simply by offering their own products at a rather ridiculously cheap amount and thereby spoiling the market.

Truly, there is a drastic reduction in energy costs, but, the complex levels for Bitcoin (BTC) mining have moved up in terms of everything it entails. Well, there is about two exceptions. The difficulty levels in Bitcoin (BTC) persistently rose over the last years.

It then increases the cryptocurrency's hash rate and it is necessary to ensure Bitcoin's (BTC) security.

Yes, and yes it costs more energy, but a significantly complex issue set translates to a more secure bitcoin network.

Dividing profit into halve as a reward for Bitcoin mining from 25 to 12.5 so as to enable the miners to work even harder to be able to earn the same number of Bitcoin (BTC) like they did before.

Then there is a particular projection, which has indeed played an important role in fueling up the prices of the cryptocurrency.

Lately, most of the miners within the cryptocurrency, have imbibed new algorithms that only need less processing power. For instance, the recent Bitcoin Cash (BCH) miners mitigate problem difficulty depending on hash rate, just to ensure that a lower power consumption is achievable.

The net effect is, directed to the energy costs and, still comprising the main components of Bitcoin (BTC) mining costs while still exerting minimal influence on its price. The energy costs relative to Bitcoin (BTC) mining activities guarantees that it remains an important barrier to enter the industry.

CHAPTER 9: Decentralized system VS Centralized system - In Contrast with FDIC traditional Banks.

I have been mentioning "decentralized network" and a centralized network".

Well, I have been working on a way I can just talk about things in clearer way. And, I would not want to talk too much about it, but it is not me talking, my hands want write so much.

A decentralized network is what is referred to as a "trustless environment," and there is no single point of failure.

All the nodes linked in the network are not even relying on a single server point and each node, undoubtedly holds the entire copy of the network configurations.

But we are talking about the decentralized system.

A decentralized system, the kind of system that is an interconnected information system, and no single entity is the primary authority. In the context of computing and information technology, decentralized systems usually exist in the form of networked computers.

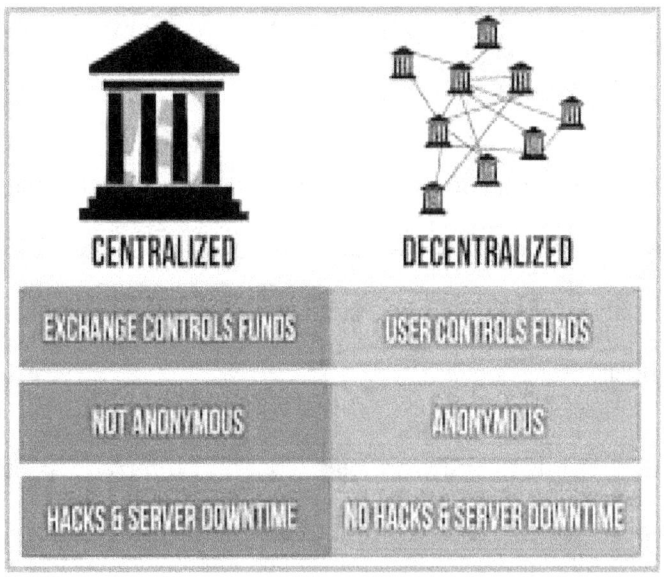

While, a centralized system is a system that uses client/server architecture where one or more client nodes are intently or directly linked to a central server. This is the most frequently used kind of system in so many organizations where a client sends a request to a company server and receives the response.

FDIC means Federal Deposit Insurance Corporation. It is a federal agency, an independent one at that. What does this agency do?

They are always insuring deposits in America and thrifts if there is any event of a bank fail.

Federal Deposit Insurance Corporation was actually created in the year 1933 in order to have the confidence of the public maintained and to be able to embrace and encourage the financial stability in the system by promoting a sound banking practices.

Federal Deposit Insurance Corporation, insures deposits of up to $250 thousand per depositor but as long as that institution is FDIC insured.

The sole purpose of the Federal Deposit Insurance Corporation is to shun "run on the bank" events, because it has been a factor that has caused a serious devastation of many banks especially during period of the Great Depression. For instance, whenever a threat of closure of is gotten by a bank, the small groups of worried customers suddenly and rapidly rushed to withdraw their money. After the fear has spread, a stampede of worried customers, seeking to do the same as the earlier group, without any further details, it has resulted in banks being unable to support any withdrawal requests. Only those who were first to withdraw their money from that kind of a troubled bank will benefit, whereas those who have waited risk

But, from the little information about the FDIC is enough to guess something

About this agency. They can do everything they want to do because they are independent.

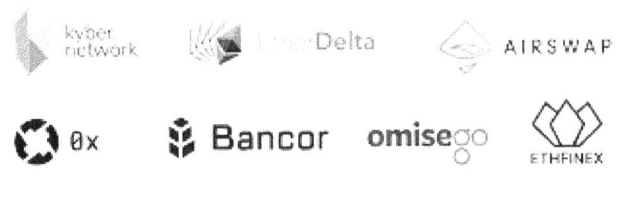
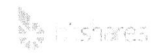

Decentralized CryptoCurrency Exchanges

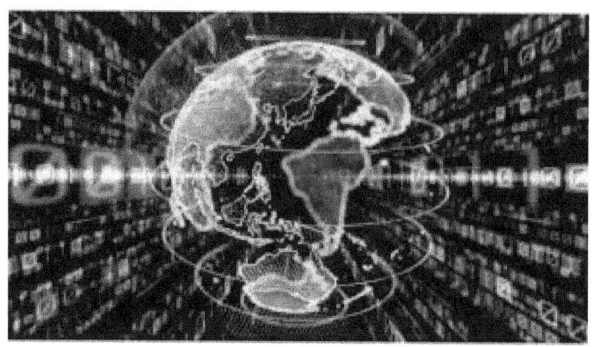

CHAPTER 10: Regulations on Cryptocurrencies - Position of some countries on the issue {XRP to be the new Euro Digital Currency} / Blockchain concept.

Every country in the globe has their distinct regulations concerning the cryptocurrencies.

But, everyone of this cryptocurrency has their own blockchain.

A blockchain is a system of taking records of information in such a way that makes it hard or so impossible to change, hack, or cheat the system.

A blockchain is technically a digital ledger of transactions that is replicated and spread across the whole network of computer systems on the blockchain.

Every block in the chain contains a certain number of transactions, and every time a fresh transaction is made on the blockchain, a record of that fresh transaction is added to each of the participants' ledgers.

A case where decentralized database is managed by multiple participants such a style is known as a Distributed Ledger Technology (DLT).

And blockchain is a type of DLT in which all the transactions are recorded and are not able to be altered in the memory after its value in relative to a cryptographic signature called a hash.

Let us quickly talk about some regulations concerning cryptocurrencies and XRP to be the new Euro digital currency.

There is no doubt that there is a wide spread of the cryptocurrencies and their acceptance as a digital currency across the globe, which has over time brought about some certain ambiguities in the areas that is encompassing their usage, operations and if course, their regulations.

A peculiar characteristic of a crypto currency transactions is, they are running through the use of a very fortified cryptography that entails unfathomable codes as they are codes.

But, the regulation of digital or virtual money varies based on the fact that all countries are entirely different and function differently.

Its status is not actually identified in some jurisdictions, while others attempt its regulation based on what they sense a cryptocurrency to be.

Most countries do not actually make utilizing a cryptocurrency illegal. its status as currency, differs in line relative to regulatory implications.

When there is no specific devoted central authority and regulation, that oversees all activities and transactions pertaining to the utility of a digital or virtual money, is what is believed that makes it vulnerable enough for anyone to use to his or her own advantage especially to carryout illegal intentions at worst, fraud.

However, a few regulations that have been made in some particular jurisdictions took a rather slow turn as most authorities wrestled with understanding a bit of what exactly the cryptocurrency technology is actually about before they can attempt to assign specific regulations to its utility and technology.

Nonetheless, despite all the moves taken, there still no uniformity as per any international approach to regulating digital currencies. Apparently, as things are, its regulation really relies more on the actions taken by each of countries of the world.

In the U.S, digital currencies are regulated through at least five (5) different Federal Agencies namely:

The Internal Revenue Service (IRS)

The Financial Crimes Enforcement Network (FinSEC)

The Securities and Exchange Commission (SEC)

The Securities and Exchange Commission (SEC)

The Commodity Future Trading Commission (CFTC)

Office of Foreign Assets Control (OFAC)

Each of these Agencies see from a very different point of view despite being all about digital money.

China being an Asian country and being one of the most populous countries in the world, prohibits the anyone from making use of a digital money. Though, this action raised a lot of controversy and resistance. But the Chinese government seem to frown at cryptocurrencies and its market with the purpose of preventing financial risks.

China wants to take down all pertaining to cryptocurrency trading with a ban on its foreign exchange.

These regulatory actions by the Chinese government are to ensure a control over the increasing mania in relative to a decentralized, non-regulated digital money.

Despite the ICO ban and momentary rejection, cryptocurrency trading is still very much taking place in China, as many participants even moved to foreign exchanges.

One of the major European central banks is reportedly eyeing Ripple (XRP) as a potential platform for issuing digital Euro.

Bitcoin (BTC) and Ethereum (ETH) being the two biggest digital money, have been observed critically.

Bitcoin was said to be a too dangerous means of exchange and Ethereum (ETH), a decentralized digital money and thus, cannot under the control of any government.

The whole world is swiftly going into a new phase of technological advancement as a to the recent global pandemic.

Ripple (XRP) is a cryptocurrency that operates on its own ledger and this simply means that Ripple (XRP) does not actually operate on a blockchain network like that, but has its own ledger for making transactions.

The cryptocurrency, Ripple (XRP) is actually very trusted by several banks as a model for CBDC as per its high centralization.

XRP has got the trust of several banks as a model for CBDCs because of its highly centralized feature, based on a network in which only certain network nodes can validate transactions.

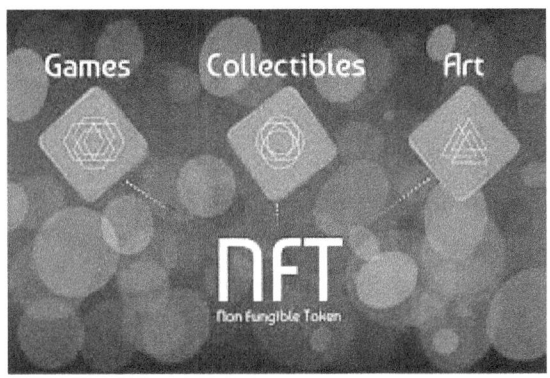

CHAPTER 11: Concept of NFT

It's natural at this point for you to be wondering " what does NFT mean?". It's totally fine if you've never heard or don't really know what it means.

So, to tackle first things first, I'll be simplifying what NFT means before we move on to shedding more light on the concept.

What is NFT?

NFT in full means Non-Fungible Token. Now, to break that down, the "non-fungible" there simply means unique or special i.e., it's a unique or special token that can't be substituted or replaced with another or anything else.

NFT In the Digital World

NFTs are cryptographic tokens that can be used to represent a particular and unique real-life item that has been digitalized. In other words, NFTs are unique digital representation and collectible of things such as artworks, audio files, videos, video games and so on. They are unique because they cannot be interchanged, neither can their ownership be affected or transferred in anyway as an NFT carries a permanent print or signature (i.e., the name of the creator) as a proof and representation of ownership from the moment it is created till forever.

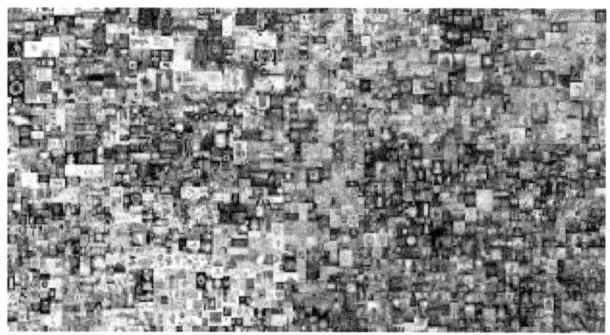

NFTs, unlike Cryptocurrencies (just like the money we spend in our real-life daily transactions) such as Bitcoin and Ethereum, is not fungible i.e., they cannot be switched or swapped neither can any two NFT be identical. For instance, a bitcoin would be exactly the same as another (1BTC: 1BTC) but with NFTs, it would not result as such because in nature they have been built differently in a way that they are outrightly not interchangeable with any other token.

Every sales transaction of NFTs are efficiently documented by a digital ledger called Blockchain. The advanced technology records all the buying and selling. NFTs can appear to be GIFs, tweets, digital trading cards, or virtual real estate, and so on. An artist can decide to make NFT of her music album instead and put it out for sale, that way she gets to own her creation and may also get direct profit from it each time it's sold to a buyer (I'll shed more light on this part as we go).

An NFT can be likened to a museum piece or original artifact or artwork such as the Mona Lisa painting that's auctioned out, pieces like this have the signature or tag representing the creator's or affirming its originality and the value of the originals is usually what would distinguish them from counterfeit and fakes, this is similar to what an NFT is and why it is collected, just that in the case of an NFT, there's no physical item, just digital. Yes, NFTs are valuables that are digital (i.e., virtual) in nature. Buyers can collect them (buy) at online auction websites or directly from the seller, keep them while they appreciate in value and decide to sell them (whether by auction or whichever way) for higher price in the future. For instance, a buyer buys an NFT of an original painting at an auction house for $9,000 dollars, then keeps it in his digital wallet for 8years while it rose in value, then auctions it out and finally sells it to the highest bidder for $1million. The whole NFT issue today might seem like a fuss but it is definitely worth acquiring. As a matter of speaking, there are predictions that you might find yourself verifying the ownership of your car, house, or so with an NFT or even have to open your door with one in the future.

The first set of NFTs appeared sometime Late in 2015 between October and November and they were mainly Ethereum based. As a result of NFT having Ethereum as its base, they are compatible with any platform built using

Ethereum and likewise can be traded on every Ether (Ethereum) marketplace. NFTs can be purchased with Ethereum or ERC-20 tokens such as WAX and Flow.

Today, there are some reservations and criticisms against the kind of blockchain system used in NFT transaction (i.e., the Proof-of-work blockchain) because of the level of carbon footprint it generates. And as it's no news that greenhouse gas emission contributes to global warming and the issue of climate change, it's definitely not nice if the system continued like that. So, in response to all these, the Ethereum foundation is working towards upgrading to a less energy intensive Proof-of-Stake validation protocol that is predicted to consume less than 1% (99.98%) of the energy the former currently uses by 2022.

How NFT works/ Its Benefits

Every Non-fungible token that exists can be traced to a creator. Any token you come across has an owner and can be verified without hassle (it is easy to verify). They cannot be manipulated or stolen. And they can be sold or resold. Also, you can own and hold an NFT forever, rest assured that your NFT collectible is secured in your digital wallet.

In some cases, the creator of an NFT earns royalties each time his/her NFT is resold. Yes, they can. Some NFTs are built to automatically credit their original creators with a certain percentage (for instance 8%) each time they are resold thus, making profit each time and as long as their NFT is being resold.

As a creator, you control and have power to determine the scarcity of your creation i.e., you get to decide how large or little the quantity of your NFT would be up for grab. For instance, like the central bank of a country prints out a specific amount of each currency note to put out for circulation e.g., producing 3 million copies of $100 notes. All the 3 million of them are originals and likewise same as all the copies of your NFTs as your signature remains unchangeable and stamped on them. Also, you get to choose to sell it on any NFT market or direct seller to buyer platform without any intermediary.

NFTs are used to maximize creator's earning, as they possess an upgraded creator economy where they don't have to dish out the ownership of their creations to publicity platforms anymore. Instead, their ownership is injected permanently into their work at the onset and remains so for as long as forever. Also giving them a chance to earn directly from the sales of their creations.

In some games today, you can now buy NFTs for you to use in them (the games). You can sell these NFTs afterwards to get your money back and might even make some profit if the item rises in value as a result of higher demand. Just as explained in the last paragraph before this, the developers of these games can also get royalties as a result of the continual buying and selling.

Whether you've heard of the news of the digital artwork of Beeple's that was sold at the auction at Christie's for US$69.3million earlier in March this year. Or maybe you've heard of the news where the CEO of Twitter, Jack Dorsey sold his autographed first tweet for $2.9 million. Or just maybe you heard of the one that happened in February this year, where a Lebron James slam dunk NFT card was sold for $208,000. Well, that's to hint you on how fast the market of NFT is growing. Though, there are criticisms and opinions that NFTs are overrated and not so smart (usually with a screenshot of an NFT digital artwork to prove their points). Some claim that it is stupid and a waste to purchase an NFT artwork for thousands and as high as millions of dollars when they can just google it out, screenshot it and own a copy. But even though that can be true, possessing a counterfeit or inferior would never feel the same as owning an original, the real piece. Take for example, in 1999, over a million copies of a particular brand of T-shirt was widely sold across the globe and you are one of those who own one, then you attended one of Michael Jackson's concert wearing this T-shirt and you were super lucky and privileged to get backstage and to get an autograph (The Legendary MJ signed on your T-shirt!!! You should probably make it a museum piece or keep it in a high tech safe or hang it on your wall for display or something!). It's no news that no matter how small or big his autograph on that copy of widely sold T-shirt, it has automatically appreciated in value more than its counterparts. From that moment, its status has changed from common to unique. Now, imagine auctioning that particular T-shirt 10years later or today. Yes! Exactly. Now you get the gist of owning an NFT. Also, the digital artwork generally appreciates or gains more value the more it is sought after, screenshot, shared amongst peers or widely used, which automatically ends up working for the benefit of the owner of the original piece if and whenever he decides to sell it out in future.

If you can become a digital artist to create digital art into an NFT. Nifty Gateway is where you can sell NFTs by auction and make Millions, in addition: in the marketplace is where Nifties are traded user to user or you can buy directly from the drop NFTs as well. This is my Golden Ticket statement for NFT.

https://niftygateway.com

There are 5 Marketplace where you can discover, buy, trade and sell NFTs:

1. Enjin Marketplace: ETH is required to process transactions.

2. Rariable: offers minting and marketplace services for NFTs.

3. Super Rare: NFT marketplace that deals with unique digital art works.

4. Decentraland: it's a fully decentralized digital world where users can purchase plots of land (NFT assets) that they can develop upon.

5. OpenSea: The first and largest marketplace where it allows users to sell art, game items, collectibles, virtual stuff, domain names etc. OpenSea focuses on every type of NFT. Browse and buy Crypto Collectibles on OpenSea. Golden Ticket statement.

My Golden Ticket recommendation for buying NFTs are from these 3 NFT makers:

1. Chiliz (CHZ) is an ERC20 utility token on the Ethereum blockchain that serves as the digital currency for the Chiliz platform for NFTs. This is my 3rd Golden ticket of choice to buy for NFT.

2. ECOMI coin: VE-VE is an app-based marketplace for premium licensed digital collectibles. With VE-VE, users can acquire common, rare, or one of kind digital art collectibles, customize and showcase NFTs in the virtual showrooms as well as sell, buy or trade NFTs amongst other VE-VE consumers from their mobile devices. ECOMI coin is my Golden ticket 2nd choice of Crypto currency to buy for NFTs.

3. Ethernity Chain: is a platform where you can explore digital art mainly NFTs. Ethernity Chain will enable users to own unique digital artworks

where they are tokenized and will be traded on the blockchain. I highly recommend Ethernity Chain as my Golden ticket choice.

CHAPTER 12: Wallets and External wallet devices - How to secure your Cryptocurrency from Hackers.

The digital wallets are where your cryptocurrencies are stored. I have spoken a little about it earlier.

A cryptocurrency wallet could be a software program, online platform or even a hardware device, that is capable of holding the keys used in order to send and receive different blockchain cryptocurrency tokens.

Literally, it is like a storehouse where your private keys and your public keys are stored alongside with your digital money. The sure way to protecting your assets is done as your wallet interact with blockchain cryptocurrency ledgers. And you can easily check your cryptocurrency balance with ease.

In this new era of cryptocurrencies, our mobile phones, hard drives or removable storages have turned into a bank vault.

This is an effect caused by decentralization, there is no intermediaries such as banks. Cryptocurrencies have actually made so many people more independent, even though it is quite a risky era we are living.

Hardware wallets are actually one of the secured ways to keep your cryptocurrency. And, they are also called a "cold storage". It is offline and it is more secure than hot storage wallets. Just be careful, do not misplace it and also work against it getting infected. Trezor is an example of a cold storage. It is bulletproof and it has a two-factor authentication, a password manager app, and so compatible with ERC-20 tokens.

Software crypto wallet could be hacked since it involves

the internet. But it is good for heavy traders. While,

App-based wallets is the best Android crypto wallet. Binance is mostly known as a cryptocurrency exchange, but it also has its official mobile app called Trust Wallet. Trust Wallet supports more than 40 blockchains, and it is decentralized.

CHOOSE YOUR BEST CRYPTOCURRENCY WALLET

CHAPTER 13: Coinbase/ Coinbase Pro — top Cryptocurrency brokers & How to buy, sell, convert, send and receive Crypto worldwide.

Coinbase is an exchange. I mentioned that earlier.

Coinbase and Coinbase Pro are both user friendly secure platforms for Cryptocurrency exchanges. Both platforms are two of the most popular ones for buying, selling, and storing Cryptocurrencies such as Bitcoin (BTC), Ethereum (ETH), Litecoin (LTC) and so on. And they're both created to make trading and investing of cryptocurrencies simple for users. Billions of dollars have been traded on both platform since the past year. These two platforms are very efficient, accessible and transparent for crypto financial transaction.

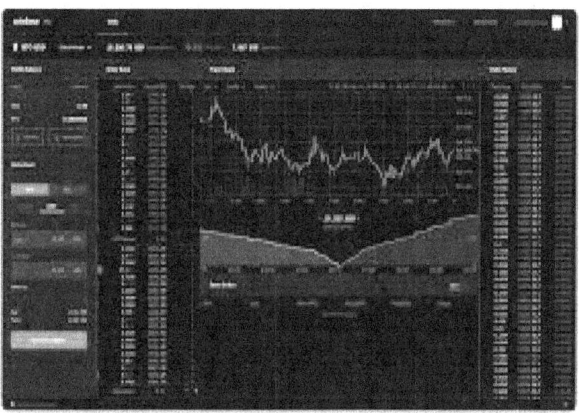

Coinbase Pro – Trading Platform

Though Coinbase and Coinbase pro are both owned by the same company (Coinbase Global, Inc.), they have been built with some differences. Coinbase was developed before Coinbase Pro and it is specifically the most suitable for new users who want to invest and make their first purchase. Coinbase Pro is a more technical one. It is designed to suit professional crypto traders more. Unlike Coinbase, it isn't really fit for beginners but for experts or the experienced traders of Cryptocurrency.

Both platforms have variety of benefits and privileges. Apart from the easy buying and selling feature, they both allow you to keep track of your digital currencies (crypto), with vault protection feature for added security, can be download as app to your Android or iOS, Cryptocurrencies stored on them are protected by the company's insurance policy, sales of variety of digital currencies, open to over a hundred countries and so much more. Both platforms are essential if you really want a clean Cryptoeconomy journey, they are very necessary to possess at one's disposal.

Coinbase IPO will be listed on NYSE NASDAQ on April 14th, 2021. Utilize Coinbase as your Crypto Currency Exchange Broker and now you can invest in your own Coinbase Wallet on the NYSE NASDAQ earning you even more proceeds on both ends. This is my Golden Ticket recommendation.

To buy cryptocurrencies

Firstly, sign in to Coinbase.

Then select Buy / Sell

Select the Buy field to pick the asset you want

Input the amount you want in crypto or your local currency.

Select payment method.

Click Preview Buy to confirm your purchase (you can always click the back arrow to make a change).

Click Buy to complete the process

Want to sell?

Select Buy / Sell on a web browser or tap on the Coinbase mobile app.

Select Sell.

Select the crypto you want to sell and enter the amount you want to withdraw.

Select Preview sell > Sell now to complete this action.

Send?

From the dashboard select Pay from

Select Send

Enter the amount of crypto you'd like to send. You can toggle between the fiat value or crypto amount you'd like to send.

Enter address, phone number or email address of the person you are sending the crypto to.

Leave a note (optional).

Select Continue to review and confirm the details of this send.

Select Preview

Select to Send on Coinbase (off-chain) or Send on the blockchain and follow the remaining prompts

Receive?

From the dashboard select Pay l

Select Receive

Once selected, the QR code and address will populate

Convert?

Sign in to your Coinbase account.

2. Click Buy/Sell > Select Convert.

3. There will be a panel with the option to convert one cryptocurrency to another.

4. Enter the fiat amount of cryptocurrency you want to convert in your local currency. For example, $10 worth of BTC to convert into XRP.

If you do not have enough crypto to complete the transaction, you will not be able to complete this transaction.

5. Click Preview Convert.

6. Confirm the conversion transaction

Moreover; here are my Golden Ticket CryptoCurrency recommendations of crypto Long and/or short-term trading/Investments that you must have when building your personal Coinbase portfolio that will make you a millionaire:

- Bitcoin, Ethereum, Cardano, Decentraland, Ankr, Chainlink, Polygon, Stellar Lumens, The Graph, XRP, Polkadot, THETA, Dogecoin, VeChain, IOTA, Chiliz, Enjin Coin, Theta Fuel, Solona, Holo, Binance Coin, Tether, Tezos, Cosmos, Compound, Stablecoins and Ethernity Chain. (basically, any ALTcoin over $3billion dollars Market Cap you should be good to go with long-term investing on that coin.)   ALTcoins will be outperforming after Bitcoin hits its peak this fall season and then all the ALTcoins will rise and go parabolic.   So now is the time to get in on all ALTcoins, be sure to check to make sure the market cap is in the $ Billions of dollars before purchasing.   Wait until the coin price drops low in price to take a position for maximum gains in October 2021.   We are following 2020 Bitcoin pattern last year where Bitcoin always peaks in the Fall season and then the ALTCoins will peak and go parabolic after Bitcoin falls. This is my Golden ticket statement for my readers.   My recommendation is to buy in now and watch your money grow in cryptocurrency 10x more than the conventional NYSE stock market. If you're a trader buy in now with ALTcoins and then get ready to sell some or all in October 2021 and thereafter. I recommend if you're wealthy stick with buying Bitcoin and Ethereum, however; if you're just starting out with less cash than going all in on the ALTcoins route will be just fine for you. However, continue to buy Bitcoin and Ethereum in fraction of a coin is fine as well. Having .01 Bitcoin will be enough to make a handsome profit.

My recommendations is that you buy at least 1,000 to 10,000 or more coins of each ALTcoin as you can, so that when October comes you can sell 10% each time the price goes parabolic or just sell it all. It depends if you are a trader or a long-term investor. But in most cases the price will go up and up and you would have already sold and wished you had held on to them longer to sell at the highest price possible, with Cryptocurrency the sky is no limit here…

Note: Bitcoin and ALTcoins do very well in the Bull Market; consequently, in the Bear market Bitcoin upholds more value than ALTcoins. So be careful if you're a trader you want to sell all in October because once the price drops in the bear market your ALTcoins will drop down to 98%.

My prediction is that Bitcoin will rise to $75k in the summer months. Word is out that Walmart the Mega Retail Store has just purchased 1 billion Bitcoin. Looks like Walmart will be accepting Bitcoin for their product purchases very soon. Which means the price of Bitcoin is going up to $75k very soon. Therefore; keep buying Bitcoin before the supplies run out as more and more retailers and corporations join in with us and buy out Bitcoin in the coming months of 2021. Bitcoin price will rise to $100k by end of 2021 and this is my golden ticket statement.

Good luck and like Mr. Spock use to say on Star

Trek; "Live Long and Prosper…"

CHAPTER 13: Own a free account today - How to Open an account with ease and get free Bitcoin for yourself and a friend.

"Go to https://www.Coinbase.com to sign up

Specify your account details, including your name and email address. You'll receive an email asking you to verify your email address

After verifying your email address, you will be prompted to enter your phone number. Please provide a mobile number as you will be demanded to verify the phone number via SMS

Depending which region, you are in, you will be asked to

provide your name, date of birth, address, intent, source of funds, occupation, and employer

Have your government-issued ID available as you will be asked to upload or take a photo of it

US and UK customers will need to complete an ID verification for documents and an ID verification for a profile

All other customers will need to verify two IDs of different types. Passport, driver's license, or government-issued ID cards are acceptable forms of ID; health cards and student IDs are not accepted

Once you verify your ID, you may link a bank account or select Start Trading to skip this step for now" Coinbase.

And remember to use my referral link below as you are registering. A benefit you don't want to miss is, you'll both get free Bitcoin when a friend buys or sells $100 of crypto by earning a Reward of $10 in BTC.

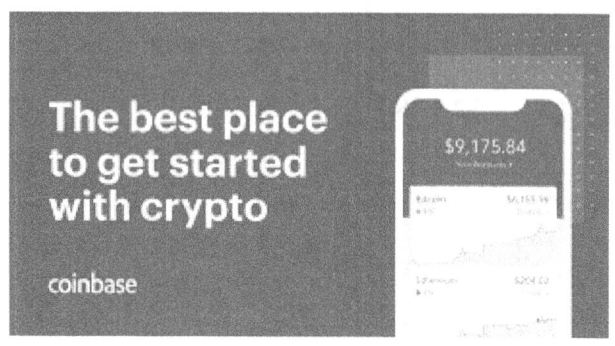

Sign up for free on my Coinbase Referral link; https://www.coinbase.com/join/alo_kw

Coinbase will give you and I, $10 dollars in Bitcoin when you sign up under my referral link. Remember Bitcoin will be $1million in 2025, so that $10 dollars in Bitcoin is a good start.

Coinbase is a secure US company based out of San Francisco a Crypto Currency Broker, currency exchange, Coinbase Pro – Trading Platform, Coinbase Wallet and Coinbase Commerce (integrates into your Shopify Store or other stores as your payment provider for Cryptocurrency; where customers can pay for products on your store with Bitcoin.) You get all 4 Coinbase Platforms where you can sell, buy, convert, send and receive crypto currencies worldwide. Now that's a great component to have all your crypto currencies all secured within your Coinbase wallet while you travel the around the world today. It's like having a your very own personal broker and currency exchange in the palm of your handheld device and in your pocket. A very great ideal concept for the avid traveler in today technological world.

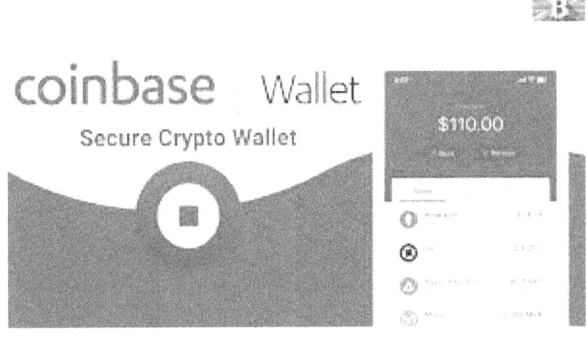

Author's Note

My name is John Alo Jr aka KAMAKIUGA (means "Junior-boy" in Samoan language). I am ¼ Hawaiian- ¼ Chinese and 1/2 Samoan, my late Mom was full Samoan from Amouli, American Samoa Islands. I was born and raised in Nanakuli, Hawaii. You can visit my Social Media to learn about me. I am an USPS Carrier Technician for the United States Postal Service. I am very real and very ambitious and I have lots of ventures that I am working on and this book writing venture is one that will be my favorite venture as a writer and author of my Kamakiuga series best-seller books. I currently live in Seattle, Washington.

And, you, are my dearest book readers and audible, you are helping me in the fulfillment of my dreams and to hopefully retire from my 30 long years of work and return to my homeland in Nanakuli, Oahu, Hawaii with my great accomplishments in achieving my Bachelors of Science Public Affairs Degree in Environmental Management from the School of Public and Environmental Affairs (SPEA) at Indiana University Bloomington, my current USPS career goals and my historical legendary aspirations….

Remember to keep your long-term investing growing in Bitcoin, Ethereum and your favorite ALTcoins in your Coinbase portfolio; because soon we all will be crypto currency millionaires… and that my friend is my golden ticket statement.

ALOHA AND MAHALO NUI LOA,

AUTHOR: JOHN ALO JR. / KAMAKIUGA

KAMAKIUGA@GMAIL.COM

Copyright: KAMAKIUGA 2021